PRAISE FOR *ℏℴ ℘ℒℴℴℴ ℴℴℴℴℴ*

"A holistic, soul enriching, and no B.S. invitation to nourish the mind, body, and spirit. Amrita's honesty, refreshing humor, and expertise reminds us that we are already whole as we take the leap towards accessible and achievable steps towards resilience."

– Heather Ridge, M.S., Licensed Clinical Mental Health Counselor

"A joyful read and delightful tool for living your most-longed-for-life. Filled with hard-earned wisdom, practical life hacks, and much heart, this book sweetly reminds us that our choices create our lives."

– Marissa Ferkovich, Artist, USMC Veteran, Elder Millennial

"A guide for anyone who desires to break free of the 'box.' Amrita combines professional knowledge of positive psychology with the wisdom of a diversified and fearless life. ...An inspiring, holistic, and accessible masterwork...instilling courage in the reader and offers practical steps for true change."

– Scott Foy, PhD, Computational Biologist

no
plaid
suits

no

plaid

suits

*how not to have a
boring, normal life*

AMRITA ROSE

atmosphere press

*"To live is the rarest thing in the world.
Most people exist, that is all."*
~ Oscar Wilde, poet and playwright

*Sometimes the thing that gets you to do the thing you really
want to do but have been avoiding for no apparent reason,
is something that kicks you in the ass, breaks your heart,
or otherwise confounds what you thought
you needed to get moving.*
~ Amrita Rose

Table of Contents

Author's Note

I asked myself, am I willing to be a mother to the world?

*Am I willing to include everything rather than
divide and conquer?*

My answer was a resounding YES!

This collection of essays grew out of a desire to share what I've learned about personal resilience, finding joy and creating a life of adventure and freedom. For decades I contented myself with teaching my students new ways to think about their lives. I worked hard to present them with fresh ideas and new challenges. I often took a devil's advocate position in arguments, all because I wanted them to see how they could grow their resilience.

Mostly it worked, sometimes it didn't. But for every

student I taught, no matter if the subject was photography or art, yoga, meditation, or general mental and physical wellness, the thing that drove me was my desire to give each person an experience of the power they have over their actions and in their own lives.

When I created my business, An Unstoppable Life, I wanted to find ways to share the knowledge and journey I'd taken. The name was important because it was, and still is, how I feel about the life I continue to create. I'm not saying that I wake up every day with a circle of bluebirds flying around my head à la Cinderella, nor that every day starts or ends as I'd hoped or desired. What it does mean is that I recognize choices and opportunities every day to transform my life. Living this way makes me feel unstoppable and I want you to feel that too!

I see each student, client, and reader who comes to me as one of my kids, and just like any mother, I wish the very best for each of you. I want you to feel brave, strong, and powerful in ways that imbue you with compassion, caring, responsibility and joy. I want you to feel ownership of yourself and understand how to create a life that feels meaningful, feeds your soul, and makes you giddy with happiness. Most of all I want you to experience what living an unstoppable life truly looks and feels like.

When you change what you believe about something, it changes the patterns in your brain and the whole world will not only appear different but will BE different.

This collection of essays is meant as a guide, maybe a map. You can read a few or all of the essays and never set foot on the path, or you can shove the whole thing in your pocket, sling your pack over your shoulder, and set off, knowing that you don't know everything just yet; still willing to have an adventure. I hope you'll be willing to explore and be open to the world you'll discover within these pages. The only thing to remember when reading this collection: be willing to try your hand at anything and everything as you find what you're best at and attend to the ones that feed your soul.

You already have everything you need. Now it's a matter of unlocking what you've secreted away inside yourself, thinking it wasn't right, or good, or enough. Because you are human, you have all the abilities to be LIFE writ bold. You are enough... ditch your beliefs, let yourself be guided by what you experience, and stop depending on the map. It's the same as walking. Put one foot in front of the other and see where the steps take you.

I invite you to be 100% willing for where this journey takes you.

~Amrita Rose

Introduction

Welcome!

I always like books that start out feeling friendly. Maybe you are stuck at home or dealing with a rapidly-changing platform at work. Maybe you're caring for family members or friends who are having a rough time. Maybe you're trying to keep your own head above water in school or work that feels challenging. Whatever your particular circumstances, this little book is here to help you. I'm here to help.

Don't panic!

First things first. No need to panic. Take a few deep breaths and dive in. I promise that increasing your resilience is not all that hard to do. It's easier than learning how to tie your shoes or make braids. It's simpler than learning to cook a turkey and far more practical. I mean really... who has time for turkeys these days?

Dive in!

Go ahead, dig in. You'll find practical information and humor, as you build your ability to bounce back and grow even in some of the worst imaginable circumstances. What you've got in hand is a compendium, a useful set of practices and ideas to help you be more resilient in the most challenging times.

Take Action!

This is meant to be a practical guide, not just a book you read while nodding off at bedtime. Read it with your morning coffee. Take one practice and try it for a week. Make some notes. Did you like it? Was it helpful? My invitation is to be curious about every idea. Play with each one. Which is most useful right now? If you like one a lot, use it more. If some don't feel timely, set them aside for later.

Play!

Your life is a sandbox and you get to create whatever you want. Sometimes kids come by and borrow your toys. Sometimes they leave their toys behind for you. Sometimes it rains, often it's sunny. Some days it's cold and you can make frozen sandcastles. Other days are hot and dry and you have to haul water from the lake to build anything. Whatever kind of day it is, this is *your* life and *you* get to choose what kind of a day you have. What do you want to build?

Not sure where to start? Well, that's why you've got this book in your hand...

SECTION ONE

You Do WHAT for a Living?

The other evening, I walked around the lake near my house with my friend Priscilla. She's smart, funny, insightful, and an ex-missionary who has a take on religion and life that's inclusive of ideas and questioning of dogma. We walk almost every week and no topic is off-limits. For example, a few weeks ago we got onto the intersection of physics, yogic science, and faith, and that conversation kept us going more than once round-the-lake.

More recently, we were listing all the crazy jobs we'd had. We discovered continuity and success, where we'd previously assumed professional disaster. We spread out the titles of our jobs like hands of five-card poker, setting each one out on the table with a story. And honestly my list looked more fit for a

Scrabble board—so many different jobs. Some intersected, and others led to new careers in unexpected ways. A few took 100% of my time and energy and I loved them. Still others I stuck with out of sheer stubbornness and in one case contrariness.

We wondered how all the experiences flowed together. How had they led us to our current careers? Looking at the crazy amalgam of job titles and descriptions, they hardly made sense to us, much less trying to explain them to anyone else. I knew that I'd always taken work that either interested me, like the R&D job working with imaging systems, or one that filled an immediate need, like the 15 weeks I worked in a sandwich shop when a semester-long class was given to another faculty member at the last minute.

Whatever the work, I always looked for something interesting in it and then tried to figure out how to do it more efficiently or "better" in some way. Sometimes that meant seeing how to make the service faster or more friendly or to make the people around me happier and feeling more supported and appreciated in their jobs. I learned something new every time and once I learn something, I ache to pay it forward.

Then...

My first real job was a weekly babysitting gig. It gave me a captive audience. Three to four evenings a week for several years I taught games with ever-changing rules, helped with homework, and created stories and plays. It fed my soul and I was got paid the queenly sum of $10 an hour. *Don't snicker, in 1977 that was twice what most 12-year-olds were being paid to babysit, and yep- we all started when we were 12 or 13!*

Though I didn't recognize it until later, all the work that followed my babysitting years involved teaching in some way. I sold eyeglasses, which meant educating people about which frames looked great or awful on them. I worked in a residential mental health center, helping residents navigate their mental health conditions with more equanimity. I also got a hell of an education from those same wonderfully generous people about what living with mental illness felt like. Not typical, but as it turned out, both jobs were incredibly useful.

I started college three years after high school. I was working for my then-boyfriend, renovating old BMW cars and old houses, when I finally got my ass to university. The guy I was dating taught me photography and inspired me to see what I could do with it and so I experimented a whole lot! Never one to follow directions once I'd learned them, I was perpetually explored alternative ways to make images. Some worked, others were terrifically messy disasters, and each one taught me something new.

I started out in the journalism department at college, as I was already spending most of my free time and money on all things photographic. I loved creating images as well as writing and I thought journalism would be a perfect combination of the two. Turned out I wasn't as interested back then in writing my way into the world as I was in exploring it visually, so I transferred to art school and the alchemy of the darkroom fed my soul. Long hours playing with crazy chemical mixtures felt like performing magic. Three decades later it still does.

The teacher in me stepped into the world without a plan. In my final undergraduate year my fave instructor, Steve, called me and asked if I'd like to teach a summer class.

I said, "Yes."

He said, "Great! It starts Monday."

It was Thursday.

I grabbed my notebooks and started figuring out a syllabus. Four days later, I was happily and somewhat nervously standing in front of 20 students. It went well, they made interesting images. I remember coming home that first day and enthusiastically ringing my dad to tell him I'd followed in his footsteps teaching art. We celebrated with pizza and a decent bottle of wine and I never looked back. I started teaching at college in 1989, before you needed a Ph.D., multiple gallery shows or publications and 25 years of experience to get hired as an underpaid adjunct. This also often meant you got to teach things you loved in exchange for being paid a pittance without benefits of any kind or a guarantee that you'd have classes the following semester. I taught as a full-time adjunct at several colleges and universities, often overlapping gigs, for more than 2 decades before moving into the corporate world of salaries and benefits packages and travel allowances.

The home I grew up in was an extraordinary place. My grandfather and father literally laid the foundation. For the most part, my parents built the house themselves, and my brother and I grew up on a construction site of constant change. Our house stood on six tree-filled acres surrounded by many more acres of forest and farmland. The gravel driveway led to a dirt road with roughly ten houses on it. We played with the sisters next door, the fearless dairy farm kids down the road, and, mostly, each other. Out of school, we wandered forest, fields, and the road; down to the creek to fish or pick blackberries. Best was the path through the woods to the neighbor who had an endless supply of popsicles and cupcakes.

Most of the kids in my school didn't spend time alone in the woods. The farm kids down the road, who appeared to live in their enormous barn, were exceptions. The fields and forest were where I felt most myself. When I was very young and couldn't sleep my dad would carry me outside into the woods. We'd listen for owls and he would tell me stories. As I grew older, I spent more and more time in the woods—that was my haven. I felt at home, limitless; surrounded by trees and sky.

Listening to the ever-present symphony; bird calls and spring-peepers, crickets, and cicadas melting in a cacophony. There were fireflies in summer sparking amid the trees. Evenings brought bats whiffling past our heads, eating the mosquitoes who made us itch.

My father taught drawing and painting at the same university where I'd go on to teach photography. My mother taught art at a city museum in the summers. My father tested out drawing assignments on me and my brother before giving them to his classes. He taught us how to use hand tools. There was always something new to learn—sharpening hatchets and knives, mixing cement, laying stone, or hammering nails. We learned new skills like how to make radio-controlled airplanes from balsa wood, how to paint with oils, fell trees, or fix a tractor.

Sometimes it was a conversation with my dad's college art students who brought the whole world of the early 1960s with them. End-of-semester student parties included music, food, and dancing from different countries; new tastes, sounds, and ideas. We were constantly pulled to expand our thinking. We were pushed to make connections between experiences. We learned a thrilling number of ways to make sense of the world. The way I was raised combined with my inner sense of exploration pretty much destined me to a life leading people to view the world in new ways.

My brother and I grew up in a home where asking questions was encouraged. The response to most dinnertime questions was a finger pointed towards the playroom/library or the fat, leather-clad dictionary on a wooden stand in the living room. A question would be asked and someone would get up from the table, lugging one book or another back to read aloud the relevant passage. Sometimes it felt like a treasure hunt, other times like an interruption of eating for a hungry kid. Learning and teaching became one and the same for me. Two ends of the same string. Before I could drive a car or cross an ocean, I was exploring the world. I also noticed that every time my dad taught, he was also filled with enthusiasm for learning.

It was a wonderful environment for growth and questioning. It was also a terrible environment for a kid who was trying to fit into typical 1960s American schooling. A notion borne out when I was asked not to return to public school for 6th grade and was "invited" to attend a Charter School instead. A turn of events I have always been grateful for.

There were things I learned not to talk about at school, like the fact that my father painted nudes, or that my mother sunbathed naked on the front lawn. Our house was set back from the road about 80 yards and surrounded by trees, so there was no way to preview what might greet me when I got off the bus each day after school. Also never mention eating calf-brain for dinners, sardines with mustard for lunch, or that I didn't like PBJ or fluffer-nutter sandwiches.

Late in my dad's life, his arthritis worsened. He'd been born during the Great Depression and was loath to spend money on things he already owned, which included drawers full of pigments, brushes, and other painting supplies. He hadn't replaced his tubes of paint in years and many had hardened beyond use. One summer he started a commissioned portrait due for presentation in September. He was frustrated because he couldn't get it to go the way he wanted. I was cleaning the gutters on the house and stopped to have lunch with him. We sat outside eating tomato sandwiches from the garden and I asked him why he was so frustrated with the painting.

After much hemming and harrumphing, he told me that he was angry he couldn't paint the way he used to. That led us to a talk about artists he most admired. He acknowledged that their techniques had changed over the decades they'd worked, and it made their work more interesting. I saw a light flickering in his eyes as he recognized a possibility for his own work to shift. He was still pissed off that his hands didn't move as easily, but he allowed the shift in perspective to happen.

We walked back to his studio and in a brash maneuver, I swept the hardened tubes of paint into the trash. My dad was speechless. I was sweeping hundreds of dollars of paint into a garbage can in front of him. We stood in the sudden silence and then he went to the drawers where he had stockpiled hundreds of tubes of paint. We spent the afternoon in his studio opening and admiring the fresh pigments. Later he turned on his music, kicked me out, and got back to work on the portrait. He'd reconnected to knowledge he'd been gathering for a decade and it propelled him forward.

The fresh palette created a connection from the past to the present. It was an acknowledgment of change. The way he was painting now was different, not worse. The stiffness in his hands forced him to change if he wanted to continue painting. Now he brought a level of insight that he couldn't have had at 20, 30, or 40. It was the kind of experience with my father that taught me teaching and learning are "go-withs." One provokes the other and both are necessary. It doesn't matter which you start with, both together are what keep life sparkling. Each time I teach, I learn something and I am absolutely hooked on the feeling.

Going back to that walk 'round the lake with Priscilla and the list of crazy jobs, sometimes it's fairly easy to see the path from one job to another or into a long-term career. Other times, well... not so much. Often it takes someone else to see how everything is connected. What I've learned in my decades as a coach and a teacher is that often we don't see the patterns we're living. It can be helpful for someone else to point them out them.

In my case, a friend named it for me when I was forty-five, working multiple jobs in a very small upstate New York town. "You show people how to see the world in new ways," declared my friend Jesse one summer afternoon as we lay on her front lawn while her two boys climbed everything in sight. "Why don't you become a life coach?" she added.

This was before there was a coach on every corner and life coaching sounded like something too vague to aim for as a career. I mentally shelved the idea until fate knocked loudly two weeks later. A yoga colleague called, she was running a final life coach training and wanted me to "round out the group." It'd be a six-month commitment of time and I'd end up with a valid coaching certification. Since I love learning new things, I figured *Why the hell not?* and said yes.

In the weeks before the first residency, I dove into the reading list, got to know my fellow attendees through e-mail, and booked a shared house in Lenox, Mass. I love learning, and life coach training was an intense blend of psychology, self-development, and teacher training. Some people took the course purely for themselves, others like me aimed to hang out a shingle as a coach at the end of the program. I felt free to explore rather than trying hard to achieve anything in particular. Maybe it was being the oldest in the group by a solid twenty years or having been invited to attend, or more likely that I was putting a whole lot of my wacky past work experience into one frame for the first time, but I loved it from the moment we started to the tears and hugs of the final day when we "graduated" each other.

Now...

Hiking takes up a fair amount of my free time. The most satisfying hikes all have sections where I think, "there is no way I'm going to make this one." Huge gravel wash-outs and crossings thick with icy mud while water rushes around my legs challenging me to stay balanced.

Once across, socks jammed onto wet feet shoved into hiking boots, clambering upwards because the path is beautiful and the day sunny. Or because the sky is clear, the air crisp and cold and I know I have a thermos of hot tea, a chocolate bar, and a book of poems in my backpack that I can enjoy once I reach the summit. Sitting atop a mountain after a difficult hike with my dog, looking out over a valley, a river, or another range of mountains is unbelievably satisfying to me. Learning and teaching are like that hike. Coaching is like that hike.

When I'm working with my clients, we traverse the path together, noticing whatever presents itself. I experience the journey while guiding my client. Sometimes it takes twists and turns we don't expect. From my vantage point, I can see hurdles often long before my clients do. In those moments, it's gratifying to know I can help them bridge whatever chasm they might come to. It's always an exploration, and it's an adventure for both of us. We're treading the same path with interwoven experiences. When you hike in the woods with someone and sit down afterward to share a drink and a word or two, you'll often name different things that got your attention. I might notice flowers, trees, and bird calls. You might tell me about the muddiness, the crunch of pine needles, or the silences.

Sharing a hike is like the twinned journey in coaching. I guide people to find whatever they love most and to learn to trust themselves doing it. I love when my clients give themselves permission to be deeply happy. Being a coach and a guide is about allowing people to see the opportunities they've missed, set aside, or told themselves were impossible. I feel a remarkable pleasure when clients allow what is possible to occur. Their faces lit like a five-year-old at a birthday party who unwrapped the most magical present in the world. That is the payoff and the gift.

Now you've got an idea of why I do what I do, let me go back to that crazy list of jobs I've held over the years...

Below is my list in no particular order:

Babysitter extraordinaire, stable help, eyeglass sales, ancillary therapist at a residential mental health center, record store employee, manager of a photo store, photo assistant, free-lance photographer, university and high school photo instructor/lecturer, A.P. art and sixth-grade art teacher, waitress, bookkeeper, shipping clerk, a technical rep for a major camera company, artist in residence, Drupal website builder, R&D for imaging systems, color management consultant, yoga instructor, meditation group leader, B&B housekeeper, dog trainer, Editor-in-Chief of a photography publication, assistant to tech company CFO, sandwich shop gal, workshop leader, drawing and painting teacher, interior design shopgirl, muralist, faux finisher, and general house painter, house and old BMW auto renovator, clothing store assistant manager, life/career/mental health coach, energy healer, public speaker, writer, singer, and visual artist.

WHEW!

Now it's *your* turn!

Now that you've read through my list—create your own.

Don't leave anything out!

Done? Great!

Go take a walk, have some lunch or a beer, dance around the room or play outside. Take a day or two then wander back through your own list.

What themes do you see? What values have you been living? Which were the jobs you loved or hated? Which was the part of either that was the opposite? What do you know

now that you didn't know when you were in the muck of it? And the final question: How does the knowledge benefit you today, tomorrow and the next day and the next...?

Career vs. Job

They aren't the same thing, though it's easy to forget this and think that your job *is* your career. If you've been feeling less than enthusiastic about what you do for work, it might be that you've fallen into the career versus job trap.

The trap occurs when you have forgotten that the job is there to pay the bills, or you've been treating your career like a job, instead of as a vehicle for your future and your passion.

Careers are passion-driven. They're the long-term series of projects which hold your interest and keep you moving forward. If you're excited by the challenges and growth, then you've got a career and not a job, (no matter what you 're doin'). The hitch often arrives when you find yourself stalled in your career because you've lost track of the challenges you wanted to meet or the future you were aiming towards.

Let's talk about jobs first, because jobs can lead to careers.

Jobs can also lead to other aspects of life that may feel more important to you than having a career, and *that's perfectly okay!*

Let's say that jobs are monetarily driven. Jobs pay the bills, keep a roof over your head, allow you to buy food, and attend occasional social events. Jobs are the training ground. They teach tenacity and perseverance. Jobs can teach you skills and launch you into the career you really want, but only if you're paying attention.

Hate your job? Fine. Jobs are like boot-camp. They can teach you the basics, often can suck, and can prepare you for a career that you really truly love, *if* you decide that's what you want.

Hang on—how is my minimum wage job at the local fast food/supermarket/gas station/strip club gonna do that, huh?

The answer is surprisingly straightforward and simple.

First, you'll need to do some work. Identify the aspects of your current job that could translate into building the longer-term career you really want. Yup! Dig in with some effort, outside of your job, after you get home, every day, probably on the weekends or in the evenings for a while. Let's be honest, creating the career you really want to take you through the rest of your life (or at least the next 20 years) is not something that you'll do overnight. If you want to sit around and let life happen to you, then you'll likely have a series of jobs and not a career. That can be okay, too.

Maybe you don't want a career. That is 100% perfectly OKAY! *And don't let anyone tell you otherwise!* If your interests in life fall in other areas, then finding work that supports those interests is the smartest thing you can do.

For example, I know a young woman in her early 30s, whom I'll call Annie. Annie is a truly gifted writer and storyteller. She loves spending time writing and telling her stories at events like story-slams. She often submits work for publication. Storytelling is her passion. She found a perfect job for herself at a legal office. She's an admin who helps keep the office running and at the end of the day she goes home, leaving work behind. She likes the people she works with and the work is challenging enough to be interesting, but it doesn't take any real creativity on her part. When she gets home at the end of the day, she pours all her creative juices into her writing. If you have a passion for creating and need time to make more stuff, then having a job that allows you the freedom of time and creativity can be a great fit. Rather than a career, Annie allowed herself to live her avocation, her passion, without the need for it to be her livelihood.

But what if I want a career?

If you truly desire a career, you can absolutely create one. The most successful and satisfying careers are passion-driven. They connect you to challenges and efforts that speak directly to your core values. This means you've got to begin by identifying your core values. Core values are the aspects of you that make you who you are. They're the types of reactions you have to external and internal events without thinking. For example, you might be someone who, no matter what, tells the truth. Sometimes it may be to your benefit, sometimes... not so much yet you go ahead and do it without really thinking about it. If this is you then truthfulness is one of your core values.

Once you know your core values, take a look at the things that interest you. What are you passionate about? What kinds of things get you excited? Remember, successful careers are created from passion + challenge + energy (effort). You've got to be passionate about the challenges a particular field of work throws your way, otherwise it's a job, not a career.

You read that right. There's no inherent difference

between a job and a career except in what you bring to the work. Get yourself clear on this and you'll begin to see all sorts of opportunities opening to you. The best part is that you'll see which ones you want to walk toward and which ones you can stroll by without regretting a single step.

What you put into it makes the difference. If you're just there for the paycheck, then you probably won't find yourself passionate or willing to put the effort into transforming your job into a career. On the other hand, if you seek out and tackle new challenges at work, and put some effort and energy into being challenged and working towards a clear outcome, then you'll likely find yourself in a career sooner than you think. Make sure that the work you're doing is aligned with who you are—with your top 3-5 core values—and you'll keep being excited and passionate about your career for at least a few decades.

Tips

◆ *For the purposes of understanding how to design your best career path, you'll want to know your top three core values and consider how you are or aren't using them in your current work.*

◆ *Notice which of your core values you lean into the most throughout your day or your week.*

◆ *What kinds of activities, whether at work or simply going about your life, feel the most satisfying to you and how do they align with your core values?*

Success

Know what you want—THAT is the key to success.

Sounds obvious but...

If your life looks great on paper and you're not feelin' it... something's off and it's up to you to discover exactly what's wonky and not working for you.

Far too often we head off in the direction of something we *think* we want only to find when we get there, that it's not *right*.

Sometimes it's only a little not right, other times it's a whole lotta wrong.

Weirdly, it's far too easy to spend five weeks, five months, or even five years working towards something you thought you really desired, only to crash hard into the wall of recognition that it's not *really* what you wanted at all.

Why does this happen?

Most of the time it's because we haven't spent any time exploring and clarifying what we truly *desire*. What specific outcome do we want to achieve? What goal do we want to reach? What need might we be looking to fulfill?

Other times it happens because we head down someone else's path thinking *that's* what we're supposed to do if we want to be successful, loved or accepted.

> *"It is better to live your own destiny imperfectly than to live an imitation of somebody else's life with perfection."*
> ~The Bhagavad Gita *by Krishna-Dwaipayana Vyasa*

Want to create real success? Start by outlining a specific, desired outcome before you take many steps forward. Create a map for yourself. Having a map lets you find/see shortcuts and ways around roadblocks when they come up.

As you travel, remember...

- ◆ It's never too late to change.
- ◆ Saying "I can't" really means "I won't."
- ◆ New actions = new experiences.
- ◆ Nothing is ever really "carved in stone".

You have to be willing to be uncomfortable in the process of creating something new.

When you choose new actions, you'll feel uncomfortable until you get used to this new way of thinking and being. Use that prickliness and resistance to reaffirm that you're on the right track. Feeling comfortable means you're sticking with what you know. To create actual change in your life, you have to do something totally new, totally different, and likely scary. You need to stretch yourself, move through your current situation, and create a new way of being and doing.

You're going to feel uncomfortable for a while... and then you won't. If you dive in and do the "new thing" with sustained effort, you create a new normal for yourself. You'll feel more comfortable as time goes on. Almost magically, one day you won't feel awkward or nervous about what you're doing, because it's simply... *the way you do things.*

Start doing things in new ways and you create new outcomes. State out loud your desired outcome or goal. Say it out loud whether anyone else can hear you or not, not matter how silly this makes you feel at first. Repeat it every day, every hour if you have to so that you don't let yourself slide into old patterns of behavior. Make it crystal clear to yourself where you're heading and what your first three actions need to be. Then... go for it and celebrate each step and each change for the accomplishment and transformation each represents.

Tips

- *Stop "doing." Whatever you're working on or wherever you're trying to get to? Stop. Don't worry, you're only stopping temporarily for a course correction.*

- *Name the three things that matter most to you. For example, community, family, security, or being healthy, freedom, and being creative.*

- *Look at what you've been doing up till now and ask yourself, "Where is what I am doing aligned with what matters most to me?" If it's not aligned, start doing something different. Aligned? Splendid! Stick with it.*

I Want It...
More! More! More!

I want it...
   If I already have it, maybe I want more of it.
   Why?
   There's no single answer, but whether you think we are driven to materialism by our culture or our nature one thing is clear. We are, at our very core, expansive beings.
   We will always crave more. More choices, more options, more ways to increase everything. We're easily caught up in thinking that by having or doing more, we will BE more. It's not true. The idea that having more makes us happier has the opposite effect. (We're not talking about the basics like food, housing, money, etc—we're talking about all the *rest* of the things we think we need.)
   Don't get me wrong, I'm not saying you shouldn't have

things. Having a place to live and a decent job are essential. Having clothes that help you feel like your best Self is a boon. Want a Tesla instead of a Honda? Bravo! Go for it. But part of expanding by accumulation is that it creates just as many restrictions as it appears to allow. Think about what you have to do to afford that shiny new car or the house with four bedrooms and five baths. Until you step back and see the actual cost of expanding this way, you won't see what your choices cost you.

For most of us, buying that newer car, a bigger house, nicer clothing, etc... costs us more time at work, which means fewer vacations, less time with family and friends, more stress, angst, worry, and less time to enjoy the stuff we have accumulated. We aren't looking at how expanding in this way places more restrictions on our freedom, time, or energy.

We humans thrive most and best when we are free to make choices. Choices help us expand into freedom. Even when we may not like either option, *we like the fact that we have a choice!* Having a choice is powerful. Having the power to choose gives our brains and our bodies an experience of creating our own future.

The big benefit is that we gain a lived sense of autonomy and confidence, and together those increase resilience. Resilience leads to courage, and courage bolsters adventure and freedom. We complete the cycle of growth by staring reality full in the face and seeking new choices. By seeing what *IS*, we are inspired to create what-comes-next rather than falling back into what-has-always-been.

When we aren't aware, we aren't able to make the best choices for ourselves. Too often we rely on old habits rather than seek new possibilities. Seeing we have a choice, we can be inspired to try something new, something different, and something creative. And that, in a word, is expansion.

The next time you find yourself craving some new thing, ask yourself, "Where is this allowing me to expand, and is this where I really want to go next?"

Time (AKA: Scheduling)

Your alarm blares and your brain kicks into high gear.

Brush your teeth, feed the kids, or the dog, the cat, or the iguana, find clothes, jump on your computer or rush out the door; whatever your morning looks like, it can feel like you hit the day running and never stop until you crawl into bed and start the whole thing over the next day.

How is it that with everything you did today you still have a huge "to-do" list and a whole pile that hasn't even made it out of your brain and onto a list anywhere? You may feel like no matter how much you accomplish there's a ton more and there is *no way* for you to get to everything you think you should do in a day, a week. Let's face it, you might often feel you'd need a free month or three to deal with it all!

YIKES!

Scheduling and "to-do" lists are only useful if they don't

terrify you. When they grow to multiple pages, or when there are a ton of "Should get done TODAY" items, you set yourself up for continued failure. The best way to get everything taken care of is to create a quick and easy system that funnels you towards completion without overwhelming you.

Having a massive daily list that includes everything you need to do can create so much anxiety that you end up procrastinating and accomplish very little except to feel frustrated or mad. By following the simple three-steps outlined below you'll make sure nothing falls through the cracks. You'll know what actions to take and you can celebrate as you knock each one off your list.

The key to getting and staying organized and on top of your life is to create a short-n-sweet system that works for you. Everyone's brain works a bit differently so you can take these three simple steps and tweak them as needed. I recommend trying it "as is" for the first seven to fourteen days before you start making adjustments. One of the biggest things that can undermine success is... our Self. Old habits and patterns of behavior can creep in under the guise of "logic" and habitual thinking. If you start with the template as it's written, you'll begin to see where old patterns and habits are hindering rather than supporting you. It's amazing what can happen when you don't act automatically and instead stretch into new patterns of behavior.

Essential Life Hack

There's an axiom in Positive Psychology that says you can change yourself from one of three access points.

1. Changing your thinking leads to changed behavior, and a changed emotional response.

2. Changing your behavior leads to a change in emotional response and thinking.

3. Changing your emotional response leads to changed thinking and changed behavior.

No matter where you intersect the cycle, you create change in all areas. Depending on what you're dealing with, one of the three access points will feel most accessible to you.

Hint: Behavior is often the easiest to start with.

Humans are notoriously poor at changing thinking and emotions right off the bat. With practice, you'll understand the relationship between the three and you can play around with all of them as starting points. I suggest going with the simplest component first and getting really comfortable with that.

Easy-as-Pie 3-Step Scheduling Template

Step 1. Do a monthly Genius Jettison.
Best done on the first day of the month. Take an hour or three (trust me—it's worth it!) and write out every last scary-huge, only-middling and teeny-weeny-winey task that needs or wants doing this month. No matter how simple or complex— if it's in your brain, offload it to your Genius Jettison List. Then go back to the previous month and add on anything left-over from the prior month. *This includes listing basics like the laundry, dishes or gerbil you have to wash, writing a daily to-do list, picking up kids or pets from somewhere, to more abstract ideas for your vacation, investment or business idea, or that poem or random quotable-quote you've had stuck in your mind. Get them all out there on paper in front of you.* Yes, I said paper! Write! Don't type! Trust me on this it's been proven to be far more effective to write than type this stuff. You can always convert it to digital later if you really really want to.

Step 2. Read through your Genius Jettison list.
Choose the three items that must be completed first and put a star next to each of the three. *Only three! No cheating!* Don't worry about whether they're large or small. On a fresh piece of paper, write those three tasks and below each one, name the first three *physical* actions you need to take to move each toward completion.

Here's an example:

Monday List:

1. *Correct blog posts from migrated website:*
    —*Pull up each post and delete any code that shows*
    —*Correct or add SEO to each post.*
    —*Double-check preview before publishing.*

2. *Do laundry:*
    —*Take laundry pile to laundry room*
    —*Separate darks and lights*
    —*Run loads, dry, and fold.*

3. *Write follow-up e-mails to business coaching colleagues:*
    —*Find contact info for colleagues.*
    —*Compose e-mail content.*
    —*Send e-mails to the 10 people on the list.*

Notice that every action is a *physical* action that I need to take, not something I need to think about. When you shift from thinking about what you need to do, to taking physical action, you remove opportunities for procrastination. One of the greatest things about being human is that once in motion we love to stay in motion. As long as you keep your attention on the action (AKA: eye on the ball), you'll accomplish the tasks you set yourself. Actions add up and pretty soon you'll have completed your daily list.

Step 3. Take a 30-second break in between items.
Do something that is physical and makes you smile. For example, walking or dancing around your office or kitchen to a fun song. By moving and giving your brain a 30-second break, you're also celebrating the accomplishment. When we celebrate, we trigger all sorts of happiness-factor chemicals to flow in our bodies and we focus on the good feelings. Whatever we focus on we create more of, so by celebrating your accomplishment you're setting yourself up to tackle the next task with an even more positive mindset and energy.

When you have completed the three tasks on your daily list, feel free to choose the next 3 tasks. Repeat steps 1-3 for the new items. In this way, you'll steadily make your way through your monthly Genius Jettison and will see real progress. Avoid adding more than 3 items to your daily list. Having three is enough and will let you track your progress rather than becoming overwhelmed, especially when the projects are larger ones.

At the end of the day take a few minutes to acknowledge what you accomplished that day.

By creating a monthly Genius Jettison, you get everything out of your mind and in front of your eyes. This frees up space for you to think, much like off-loading old files from your laptop to your external hard drive. Human brains work better when they're on task rather than distractedly trying to track and organize all the things that need to happen in the future.

As you create and complete daily to-do lists, cross the items off your monthly list as well. If new things come up as you go through the month, add them to the bottom of the monthly Genius Jettison.

Each morning, take 5 minutes to review the entire Monthly Genius Jettison, choosing only the top 3 things that have to happen that day. This way you stay on top of things and track your progress in a way that boosts celebration and accomplishment. At the end of the month, transfer anything important that must get done to the new Monthly Genius Jettison. You'll start to find that some things have resolved themselves and others may no longer be relevant. Cross those items off the list and drop them from your mind.

Do this consistently and you'll never worry you've lost track of something. You can always cross out items on your list, either because someone else handled it or because it's no longer necessary.

Tip

♦ *If your project is large or complex, it may take more than three action steps to complete. That's okay! Just start with the first three actions, complete those and then write in the next three actions you need to take. The great thing about tackling a project this way is that as you complete the first three actions, the next three become easier to plan. You may even find yourself seeing new options and shortcuts. Remember it this way: "Sets of three let me see."*

SECTION TWO

A Life Well-Traveled

Part of why I decided to write this book was to share what I've learned through all the traveling I've done. Many people have traveled more and to far more exotic places, yet when I tell people that I've moved roughly every four years since I was nine, I'm met with surprised dismay or excitement, depending on who's doing the listening.

I never planned to move quite so often but so far; I haven't found the place that feels like home. I may never find it and that's also okay. Moving to a new town, new state or even a new country has always brought me opportunities for expansion and reinvention. I get the chance to start with an open path ahead and to reinvest in the parts of my life that are truly important to me, discarding the clingy bits that seem to accumulate no matter how I periodically shake them off.

Creating home-base in a new place lets me reevaluate my

life. It's not that the opportunity to do that hasn't been there all along, but when I move far away from a place I've come to call "home," I'm called to action in ways that can offer more challenges than when I stay in the same place.

So far, I've lived in nine states and two countries: Rome, Italy (at two different times of my life); Washington, D.C.; various towns along the Delaware River; along the Hudson River in Nyack, NY and north in the heart of the Adirondacks, (a move which let me escape to Montréal many weekends); coastal New Hampshire; western Massachusetts; Asheville, NC and now, in Colorado.

Each time I've said goodbye to a group of friends, fellow musicians, artists, cooks and coffee-sharers. Each time a few of them have stayed in contact, a few have gotten pissed at me for leaving and many have simply fallen into my past (or I've fallen into their pasts, I haven't yet figured out which way that really goes).

Every move also brings in new people. A few to bike, hike, or share coffee-talk with. My recent move this winter introduced me to a hearty gang. We meet around a fire pit, enjoying the snap of early morning sub-20° Fahrenheit air, the wave of heat from a fire, and meandering conversation as a way to start the day.

I often throw potluck dinners as a way to make new friends. When I moved to Nyack, NY, to be married, we lived on a street with 17 artists. The very first week I set out to meet them. We invited all of them to the first potluck and it was such a hit, we did it again every month or so until we'd created a core group of friends. My potluck habit often morphed into an old-school cocktail party which let my more introverted side have fun, knowing I'd only have to be "on" for a couple of hours. The best part for me was introducing people to each other. Deep friendships instigated by a hot dish and a cold drink.

Sometimes dinners were small, as with the group of inventive people I became friends with in Keene Valley, NY. It was a town of 200 year-round residents and very long, snowy winters. I moved there shortly after my divorce and had planned to stay only a year, making art, teaching yoga, and figuring out what to do next with my life. I ended up with a boyfriend, four jobs, a core group of very sweet friends who saw me through the death of my father, the end of a romance, and whatever else life tossed at me. Often this involved long hikes, snowshoeing, shared meals, and several attempts at teaching me to rock-climb (a thing I'm 100% game for and only 30% good at).

Some potlucks were large and lasted so late into the night that I swore off them for months. My monthly potluck in Asheville, NC, started with 10 people and bloomed into the 50 who stayed one summer evening until I had to kick them out at 2:00 a.m. I invite people over with the words, "Bring a dish, a bottle, and an instrument if you play one. If you don't play anything I'll give you spoons." This usually ensures great music, lots of interaction, excellent food, and more laughter and connection than I can imagine building in a year of casual meetings.

I've learned to handle friends who can't bear my departures. I understand the pain that can come when a friend decides to move hundreds of miles away. When we live close to each other, it's easy to form friendships based on shared activities—hiking, walks, movies, meals. The separation created by distance shifts relationships. Like salt-water taffy, sometimes they stretch and grow smooth, other times they tear and separate.

Some people have cut ties entirely with me when I leave a place. A few will tell me in person. Occasionally someone will see it as a betrayal of friendship. Over the years I've worked to ease the pain of separation by connecting in letters, e-mails, and calls. I've also come to terms with the fact that some people will not forgive me for leaving and I have to release them with grace.

With each move, I needed to settle into a new home. When I was a kid and we moved to Italy, I looked for the shops that had the best little cakes, books, café latte, and art supplies. As an adult, I had to find plumbers, repair shops, and lumberyards. I needed to figure out who to call to get utilities turned on or off and where the libraries, DMV, and voting places were.

This often lands me in lengthy, interesting conversations. The IT guy who writes sci-fi novels and is one of the funniest people I've ever known, an English teacher whose way with poetry and narrative is equaled by a bell of a singing voice. I've been hired to do what I considered "left-hand" turns in my professional life, like building websites or helping design and build imaging systems for a major corporation, all because I asked someone somewhere a single question.

Sometimes conversations lead me directly to what I was seeking, like the best guy near Portsmouth, NH, to install my backup generator, the quietest person in the mountain town who will take me hiking, or someone in NJ to fix the clutch on my motorcycle. Other times I've learned about collecting rare books and been invited to join a writing group, teach a drawing class or jam with fantastic musicians. I can never guess what's going to come out of a conversation when I start by asking, "Where's the best place for doughnuts?" I do know whether I get the answer I'm looking for or an in-depth description of the ten best places for baked goods, whoever I've asked has an interesting story to tell, as long as I'm willing to listen.

Listening, asking questions, and getting my introverted arse out there whenever I can has made my life far more interesting than I could've imagined. It's led to jobs I never expected and adventures, travels, and romances with people and places who surprised me. My ideas about who I am and what I'm capable of got stretched and made me grow in ways I never imagined. It will do the same for you if you let it.

This book is an invitation to put yourself out there and try something new, whether it's a new place to live, a new place to hang out, new foods to taste, or new music to listen to. Ask people you don't already know interesting questions and then stick around for the real answers. All of these explorations will change you in some way—each can pull you forward and expand your world a bit more.

When you do push forward, I recommend that you allow time to breathe in the changes. Sit somewhere calm and quiet and reflect on what is new in your life. What cool, interesting, or unexpected thing happened this week, or in the past month? How did it affect you? Thoughtfully consider the changes you notice around and within yourself—this deepens and encourages more growth. It will lead you to your most enriched and authentic self, as Seth Godin puts it, "our most considered self" and a considered, authentic self is infinite, eternal, and whole.

Practical Stuff

My father took for granted a plethora of skills that few people have in our current world.

Skills are abilities and honing your adroitness in the following areas will make you a much more interesting and interested person. You'll win friends, influence enemies, and generally discover the world to be a helluva lot more fascinating place than you previously thought.

Many of these may seem overly simple. Try them anyway. If they're things you already know how to do, approach them with fresh eyes. What nuance could you add to how you already do each? More often than not you'll discover that the concentration required develops into fascination and you dive deeper into delight.

1. Learn to read a paper map correctly. Yes... REAL-LY! Increase your sense of direction with this skill and

you benefit by making quicker and more efficient use of GPS. You can be far more adventurous when you know how to read a map. There are still many exotic places in the world where GPS doesn't work (like deep in the state of Maine and lots of places abroad). You can go "off-grid" and untethered when you've got a physical map in hand.

2. Learn to drive a "stick-shift" (manual transmission) car. Especially if you like to travel! Manual drive cars dominate the road in many parts of the world. New vistas open to you when you travel this way. You gain freedom, and your critical thinking improves as you find yourself able to drive almost any type of motor vehicle. Your brain will thank you for adding new muscle-memory skills which can help ward off Alzheimer's and, as a boon, you save money (manual transmissions cost less to purchase and often get better gas mileage). Who knows? Stick shifts just might experience a nostalgic resurgence similar to the one currently happening with vinyl records.

3. Learn to read a compass. Like reading a map, you'll have far more freedom and understanding of the world when you can do this. The app on your phone will be fine for this—but learn to use the handheld plastic kind you can hang from a backpack as well. Use your new skill to find the best location for camping, position your houseplants to gain sunlight or shade, find the eastern wall, and set your bed there for great sleeping or feel more confident when setting out for a hike or bike ride in a new area.

4. Learn to read a ruler. Seriously, this is something they used to teach in grade school (along with writing in cursive), and it's one of the most practical things

you can know. Take the time to learn both inches and metric and you gain a more intuitive sense of the relationship between the two. This makes repairs much faster and simpler when you can rapidly translate one size to another. You'll be learning a new spatial language.

5. Speaking of cursive—learn to write in it. Being able to write in legible cursive is a skill that builds hand-eye coordination better than anything else. Once you can write it, you can read it—now's the time to go through all those old letters you found in that trunk in the attic. Don't have an attic? That's okay. Explore any number of antique stores or markets and astound your friends by reading inscriptions on old photos and old books.

6. Learn to properly use and care for knives. When you use and sharpen blades of any kind, you increase your proprioception, better your hand-eye coordination, and up your cooking skills. Trust me, it's far easier to succeed with intricate recipes when you're confident that you can mince and chiffonade with the best of 'em. The food you prepare, gifts you wrap, scrapbooking you do, all will feel more thoughtful and professional if you know how to use kitchen, art, or other types of bladed tools.

7. Learn how to use a hammer and saw. Again, the hand-eye coordination alone is worth the practice. Knowing that you *could* build something, even if you never do... priceless. Also, you greatly reduce the chance of injuring yourself at some point.

8. Learn to sew. No, I'm not suggesting you start making your own clothing, though you could... I'm saying that when you learn to properly use a needle

and thread, you'll repair things and feel a real sense of satisfaction, rather than tossing out that favorite shirt or pair of running shorts. Not to mention, long winter evenings can be more interesting when you're trying to darn a pair of socks.

9. Learn to read poetry out loud. Sounds totally old-school, but when you read aloud you gain way more than you bargain for. You become a better speaker, especially if you read to other people. You'll feel empowered and more capable of addressing larger groups of people. You'll develop an ear for good language and for how to turn phrases that stand out. Lastly, you'll develop your imagination and deepen your understanding of the way the world works and the way you perceive reality. Read one poem a day out loud for the rest of your life and you'll enrich your mind and your life in fabulous and as yet unimagined ways.

Tips

♦ *Maps allow you to plan adventures and be inspired. Buy some maps of places you've never heard of. Lay them out and imagine traversing the land. Allow yourself to explore by researching the intriguing places you encounter on each map.*

♦ *About using a compass: knowing how to do this is also helpful if you want to Feng Shui your house, pray to Mecca, or know the best location to plant a garden.*

◆ *Learning to write cursive increases your fine motor-skills, and improves neural connections that typing doesn't. It improves the interplay between the left and right hemispheres of your brain so you think better and faster. It helps with the retention of learned materials and allows you to read anything and everything more easily. Writing cursive also improves your ability to learn, especially if you're dyslexic, dysgraphic, or suffer from ADD or ADHD. And finally, it can increase your self-respect.*

◆ *Knowing how to sew directly translates to not having to toss things out when they have holes in them. Retooling and repurposing are the best form of recycling. Sewing also provides you with some basic first-aid practice for stitches—should you ever need to save a life or limb in that way.*

Learn to Change a Tire

Even if you always have your mobile phone.

Even if you don't have a car.

Because you ride in cars and one day you'll be in a car. It'll be dark. The tire will go flat. It'll probably be raining heavily because that's a thing that happens when you get a flat tire.

Because when you get that flat in the rain at night, you'll be outta cell service range, or your phone will have died. You'll be on a road without many other cars, or a highway where everyone's going 80mph and won't stop to help you.

Because knowing how to change a tire is not just about knowing how to change a tire, it's about knowing you can take care of yourself. Changing a tire is proof of self-sufficiency. You'll feel better about yourself if you know that you can confidently change a tire.

You'll feel amazing and heroic if you have to do it at night, in the pouring rain, on a road in a foreign country where no one else is around and you're trying to get to your Airbnb before the owner locks the doors for the night. These feelings triples if you're with someone else who does not know how to change a tire.

You'll gain a deep sense of accomplishment and be willing to tackle all sorts of new tasks. Doing so feels brave and courageous and you'll notice yourself expanding your abilities and feeling more confident.

All because you learned to change a tire.

Tips

♦ *If you don't have a car, find a friend with a car, make an afternoon of it and both of you learn together. Have fun, bring a picnic and go to the beach or the park afterward to celebrate your newfound know-how.*

♦ *Before you begin, read the manual for the car and make sure you have the proper equipment. Check to see if you need a special wrench/crowbar or locknut to remove the lug nuts that hold the tire to the rotor; most cars come with this in a kit that is stored with the spare.*

♦ *Be sure to block the wheels (front or rear) before you start, especially if you're on a hill! You do not want the car rolling off the tire jack and onto you.*

Ready To Face the Day

Way back when my grandma was a kid, "getting ready" meant being clean-shaven if you were a guy, and being "made-up" with a carefully created "hair-do" if you were a gal. There are of course plenty of examples of what being prepared for the world meant in the '40s, '50s, and later, but these days what I think being "ready" really means is showing your best self to the world in ways that *inspire* you to greater confidence *and* creativity.

"Getting ready" has always reminded me of something my grandmother constantly tried to get me to do... namely, wear dresses. She'd look at me, her 13-year-old skateboarding granddaughter, in my ripped jeans and muddy sneakers, and a loud sigh would escape her lips. Then she'd suggest we go shopping—something that I liked on par with going to the dentist to have my braces tightened. In her mind, I was the

53

very opposite of "dress for success" or "sweet young girl." In *my* mind, I was dressing like the adventurer and free-thinker I was.

Things have changed since then —I think for the better. And... good preparation is still something that is helpful and useful for us all to pay attention to. Getting ready is really about finding ways that inspire us as we show up in the world. These days that often means how we show up on a video chat, but it's all the same thing in the end.

Notice that earlier I said, "inspire you." Yes, you can dress in expensive clothing and spend crazy amounts of money on haircuts, shoes, and accessories—but all of these are really only about you feeling confident and creative in who you are.

Check out Instagram, TikTok, or any number of social media outlets, and you'll find a ton of amazing people who break the rules about what well-dressed or well-groomed is and all of them do so in service to being authentically themselves.

The point is not to dress to impress others— instead, dress to impress and inspire yourself.

It's a truism that when interviewing you always want to dress for the job you want *next*, not the one you're interviewing for. The same rule can be applied with great usefulness when you dress to impress yourself. The trick, as it were, is based on the same idea as "acting as if..." and it honestly works!

Here's how. *Bear with me for a teeny tiny bio-science lesson.*

We humans perform actions based on one of three internal stimuli: our emotions, thoughts, and habitual behaviors. Change any one of the three and you'll change the others by default. They directly influence each other. This means we can shift all three by changing just one! Generally speaking, the easiest one to change is behavior. *Face it... how many times have you said you were going to remember to be or think in some new way and then promptly forgotten to do it? Hello? New Year's Resolutions?*

By acting "as if..." we get our feet moving in the direction we want *before* we think or feel about it. By the time the mind and emotions catch up we're already acting the way we want to *be* in the future. For example, if you're an introvert and you want to be more extroverted, the first step you can take is to think of an extrovert you know and/or like being with and then do something that person would do; for example, talk to someone in line at the coffee shop or say hello on a group Zoom call if you'd normally stay quiet.

Conversely, if you often find people are put off by your extroverted high-energy and razzmatazz approach to the world, you may want to explore some behaviors of more reserved and quiet introverts. Remember that when fishing, you catch more fish by being still and quiet than by dancing on the riverbank of enthusiasm.

By acting "as if..." you're sending the signal to your brain that says, "I am extroverted, introverted, funny, joyful, silly, serious, calm, etc... because I'm acting in a way I know to be extroverted, introverted, funny, joyful, silly, serious, calm, etc...." Your brain takes it from there, flooding your body with chemicals that support the feeling of be-ing whichever way you're choosing to BE in the world. So long as you reinforce the behavior, you'll eventually *become* what you're emulating.

When you apply this trick to how you show up in the world, you'll experience firsthand how dressing and acting aspirationally helps you present your best and, surprisingly, your most authentic self. By bolstering your confidence and allowing your creativity to come forward, you bring your truest Self to the world and show off your talents and abilities in the best way possible.

Tips

- *It also strikes me as a weirder and more useful version of the old saying: "Don't screw up your face like that, it'll stay stuck forever!" In this case, getting ready consciously creates a change in how you experience the world by shifting how you show up for it.*

- *My fave right now on Instagram (IG) is @Pattiegonia, who is generous, lovely, brave, and gloriously, authentically her/him/zii-self!*

Note, while this has been proven by tons of Positive Psychology and Cognitive Behavioral Studies, it probably won't take you from being totally introverted to being Tony Robbins or from being Mr. Personality to the Buddha, but hey—ya never know!

Open a Bank Account

Actually, open two bank accounts. It doesn't matter if both are checking, savings, or one of each. Choose accounts that won't cost you anything to keep them open. Pair them so you can move money from one to the other easily, from your phone, without having to think too much.

Designate one for your living expenses (meaning monthly bills) and the other for your savings. Ideally, each week deposit between 25% - 50% of your total income into the savings account. The rest is what you have to live on and yes, this includes rent. If you can share a house or, better yet, rent out part of your home on a short-term basis, you'll knock down the single biggest expense most people face, i.e., "housing costs."

At the end of each year, transfer all but the minimum cash needed to avoid fees and keep your savings account open, into some mix of boring, stable, and solid investments. Remember you're in this for the long haul and not the fast cash *just yet.*

If you do this consistently, in approximately ten years you'll have enough to stop working just to pay your bills and you can start to do things you love, for money, *or not for money.*

The whole point is to provide yourself with an ongoing passive income through your investments so that you can spend time on things that really add to your quality of life. Owning the most *things* won't do that, no matter how much you think they will. Having experiences are what we humans crave most and experiences that involve other people nourish and enrich us immeasurably. Start collecting experiences rather than things. Celebrate your adventures and the connections you create as you grow your BTDT (Been There Done That) list.

Tips

♦ *Most banks run promotions that can earn you extra cash. Before you open any accounts, ask what promos they're running and <u>read the terms carefully</u>. Hate the bank? Once you have fulfilled the terms of the promotion, you can always take your extra cash and close or move the accounts to somewhere you like more—or another bank with a new promotion.*

♦ *Get a bank that has local as well as decent online and free banking services. You don't want to get hit with unexpected service fees.*

- *Investing can take many forms, from buying stocks and bonds, index funds, an IRA, and real estate investments... Do your research carefully and consider what form of investment is best for you once you have some general understanding of investing in general.*

- *You can also start a passive or nearly passive income stream by selling off objects you have that you no longer use, or things or services you create (à la Etsy or Fivvr). Consider what you want to aim towards and then seek patrons from Patreon, crowd-funding, or offer a subscription service for something you adore providing, Say... "Tips for better houseplants."*

Be Organized

Clean up your stuff.

Seriously, it's time!

Don't have more "things" than you really make use of.

Put them away when you're done using them.

Keep them clean and when they get too tatty or worn, fix them. If they can't be fixed, find a new use for them. If they can't be re-used somehow—toss or send them to recycling. You do not need to keep them around.

It's fine if you keep a small-ish stash of general "maybe-I'll-need-this-sometime" items. Things like rubber bands, wire ties or extra shopping bags, etc. But only hang on to what you'll make use of in a year—18-months tops. (NOTE: hobby supplies are exempt from this rule).

Keep tabs on what you've got and horizontal surfaces free of clutter. Organize drawers and closets so you track any build-up of unused and unnecessary items. Rule of thumb: If you can't see it, you'll probably forget you own it. If you don't remember that you own an item—like the retro baby-blue 1950s hand-crank ice cream-maker, the neat-o electric bread cooker, or the super-duper set of chisels you bought and put in a drawer—it is clutter.

Clutter is bad. It's hard to think well in a cluttered space. Clutter cuts down on space to dance or practice those handstands you've been wanting to perfect. Clutter can take over and you'll have less space to live and enjoy yourself. And... the whole point of being alive it to enjoy life, not to be swamped by clutter.

Tips

◆ *Go through your closets once a year. If you haven't used or worn something in a year, put it in a box and store it away with a note taped to the outside of the box that says:* **Donate or Sell This Stuff** *and date it one year from when you box it. Over the course of the year, you'll pull out anything you really need to use. Anything left in the box at the end of the year you probably don't need to keep. How do you know you won't need it? Because you did not need it for an entire 365 days.*

◆ *When my father died, we had to clean out his house. He was a child of the Great Depression of 1929 so he kept stuff because "I might need it in the future." Sounds sensible and it is—until you find yourself filling every nook and cranny with things you "might need." No one can use 1067 wire-ties or 467 pens. Trust me on this. Do a big clearing every year, you'll thank yourself. You can't take it with you and really—why would you want to, anyway?*

♦ *Pro tip: Time your once-a-year clear-the-house with spring for a fabulous yard sale and you'll double-dip the benefits. Donate what you can't sell and take the tax write-off for your donation straight to the bank.*

Make a Home for Yourself

Make your house or apartment a *home*. Create a haven for yourself.

A house is a structure. A home is a refuge from the world. It's not the place itself, it's the feeling you get walking in the door. You're in charge of creating this for yourself.

One way to feel *at home* when you're at home is to de-clutter. I know, it gets said a lot... and there's a reason for that! Having a clean and clear space around you feels calm and relaxing. When your place isn't filled with stuff (AKA: tchotchkes), your mind has a chance to rest. More stuff to look at means more input for your mind and that means you aren't giving yourself a break.

If you like collecting things, excellent! Collections can spark new ideas and remind us of pleasant things, special events, or people we care about. Set up specific areas to house your collections and make sure they stay dusted and clean. No use collecting things if you never stop to admire them. Don't allow your collections to take up more than 1/3 of your living space. Clean them, rearrange, and winnow older items as you add new ones.

Your home should reflect you and your personality. The biggest error people make is to decorate their house in a way that might look fab but isn't really you.

It's fine if you check out 'zines and sites for inspiration, but before you go styling your house from a collection of images you found, ask yourself: what are the top three things that are truly important to me? For example:

Is your job stressful and you want to come home to a calm and relaxing space? If so, choose softer-edged furniture and create a less crowded space. Clean lines and softer shapes will help you feel more relaxed from the moment you walk in the door.

Are you always creating something new and want to stay inspired? Choose brighter colors in bold hues to help you sustain energy and creativity.

Take time to connect with who *you* are at your core... then create a space that supports what you need most. No matter what, don't get suckered into decorating a room or your home because that's "what's in" at the moment. Remember, anything can be fashionable but not everything fits who you are or what you need to feel happy, content, and supported.

The truth is that no matter how wonderful something looks or how many memories it might hold for you (Great-gran's rocking chair, Mom's China set, or Uncle Bill's recliner and dartboard, anyone?), if it doesn't support who you are and what you need, then ditch it and honor your most authentic self.

Tips

♦ *Not sure if something is really you? Snap some photos or grab screenshots and print them out. Pin them up in the space you're thinking of and live with them for seven to fourteen days. What do you notice when you look at them? Do they really inspire the feeling you want? If so, go right ahead and acquire that item or something like it. Not so much? Toss the ideas that aren't working and experiment with something else.*

♦ *Remember: nothing's carved in stone. You can try things out, see how they feel, and always, always, always change them, move them, return, sell or donate them. When you find an item that now feels like a mistake, call it "practice" and move on. The only way to figure out what you really need and want in your home is to see what is not working and then change it for what does work.*

♦ *For larger purchases, spend time digging into these three key questions:*
> *Do I need it?*
> *Does it support how I want to feel?*
> *Can I really afford it now or can I save for it?*

These questions will help you make purchases that support you being your most happy and authentic self.

Housekeeping

Housekeeping is one of the most basic things you can do for yourself. Whether you rent or own your home, keeping house sets you up for all sorts of success in other areas of life. Housekeeping is more than keeping your place clean and organized—though that is a large part of it. Keeping house can be a demonstration of what you think of yourself. How you value your Self is often reflected in how you create and maintain your living space.

Let's talk about basic housekeeping and what you'll need. You can get all fancy if you love gadgets but honestly, the more machines, buckets, brooms, and cleansers you have, the less likely you'll be to use them and they take up valuable space! Better to have a few basic items that are multi-purpose than a bazillion fancy-ass cleaners, mops, or brooms.

The only tools you really need to keep any house clean,

healthy and organized are the following: a canister vacuum, a dust-pan and broom, a bucket, rubber gloves, at least two "scrubby-style" sponges, a few old t-shirts, rags or dishtowels and a roll of paper towels.

As for cleaning products, you can buy a million specialized cleaners but all you'll ever really need is vinegar, baking soda, salt, an oil-based product for wood (like Murphy's Oil Soap) if you have wooden floors or furniture, and something like Pine-Sol or another concentrated cleaner/disinfectant.

Don't want a DIY solution? Get one bottle of glass cleaner for any reflective surfaces, and one bottle of all-purpose cleaner for everything else except your wooden floors. Find a decent cleaner for wood to keep floors and furniture looking their best.

Set yourself a schedule for cleaning that you can follow, whether that's one day a week for everything, or spreading the tasks over a couple of days. The point isn't to make yourself crazy by being rigid, it's to create a system that works for you. Maybe you vacuum every other week, clean the kitchen and bath every week and figure the rest out monthly. The key is to decide and then follow through with action. *Hint: I stick notes on my fridge to remind myself.*

Not sure how often to clean? Try out your new schedule for a month, see how it feels to you, and make adjustments for the next month. If you really stick to your schedule, you'll create the perfect one within the first 90 days, and from then on, no need to think about it. Just do it!

Tips

◆ *Having spent three years housekeeping a B&B lodge, I recommend canister vacuums because most come with attachments for hard flooring as well as carpets, crevices, and furniture. They're often lighter weight and more versatile than an upright vacuum.*

◆ *This is a basic list. You can always buy a variety of specialized cleaners if you like, but if you want to save money and storage space, this list will get you through most regular cleaning around your home.*

Laundry

Yes! Laundry!

Keep reading... even if you think you know about laundry there may be some secrets hidden here. Laundry is one of those easily overlooked topics.

I understand—how exciting could a pile of dirty clothes and towels really be?

Laundry is so much more than just our dirty clothes. It's the history of what we do, how we spend our days, and how we think about ourselves. Laundry holds our (dirty) secrets. From drips of wine on a shirt to the smudge of oil on a pair of jeans, our entire daily life is written on our clothing as much as on our own skin.

What's in your hamper right now? Do you even have a hamper, or are you someone who tosses things into a pile at the bottom of the closet until the pile is too big to ignore or find your shoes under? Do you throw everything straight into the washing machine at the end of the day? Does everything go in until the machine is packed full? Do you have to haul it to the basement of your building, take it to the laundromat or drop things at the dry cleaner?

Let's get this part out of the way first: How you treat laundry is a gauge of what you think of yourself. Our clothes are one of the biggest forms of self-expression we have. They tell the story of who we think we are or—if we're really conscious of it—who we'd *like* to be.

Often, the way we dress and the way we treat our clothing is a giveaway of how we think about everything including ourselves.

Think about what you wear and how you treat your clothes. How are they a reflection of who you *think* you are or who you aspire to be? When you take a stroll through your laundry pile, what does it tell you about the person who created it?

A couple useful tips about how to treat your clothes and yourself like the functional adult you can be:

First, separate clothing into Light and Dark. *Yes, it matters*. If you want your clothes to look their best for a long time and you to look your best, you want the lighter stuff staying light and bright, not dingy because your jeans or that new blue shirt bled into your whites.

I wash everything on the Cold/Cold setting. I find it keeps all my clothing looking colorful and bright for the longest period of time.

You don't need the most "powerful" detergents on the planet and you don't need to pay extra for all the fancy-ass flavors either. Just get some basic eco-friendly laundry soap. It doesn't matter what kind you get so long as it doesn't irritate your skin, make you sneeze, or annoy your friends when you sit next to them.

If it says "dry-clean" on the label, take it to the cleaners if you can afford it. Otherwise, there are home dry-cleaning sheets you might try—do be careful: It's generally worth it to have "dry-clean" clothes handled professionally.

The most important thing is to read the labels when you're buying items and read the label again the first time you wash them. If it says "line-dry" *do not under any circumstances* throw it in that heated dryer of yours or you'll turn that gorgeous item into a Shrinky-Dink faster than you can say "Oh-shit-I-just-spent-half-my-paycheck-on-that!"

Last thing: Do your laundry on a regular basis. Don't let it pile up, because just like plates in the sink, bathtubs that haven't been scrubbed in months, and rabbits left unchecked, they seem to multiply exponentially and everything feels harder to deal with after a month or three.

Use wash time to do something fun, interesting, or productive. Whether you're doing it at home, or have to hit the laundromat, grab a book, your laptop, or your phone with that book or game you've gotten hooked on and give yourself some educational, or purely fun time. You could work on something you have been putting off and "meaning to get around to" and you'll feel like you're killin' it when you have both a finished task and clean laundry at the end of two hours.

Tips

♦ *Try a couple of mid-priced detergents out before you invest in the giant-size container. What you want is something that works well in cold water (not all of them do) and doesn't leave you itchy.*

- *Don't put anything with glitter, beads, or hand-sewn items into the washer or dryer—just suck it up and take those to be professionally cleaned. Treat them like the gems they are and you'll have them for decades.*

- *Of course there are exceptions, but the majority of people dress more or less from their point of view of the world and who they are. It can also reflect how slammed for time you may be.*

- *I am a fan of eco-friendly suds so check those out first. Most stores have their own versions which work well and are less pricey than the named brands.*

Healthy Eating

Most likely you're going to hate me for this one.

Not because I'm going to tell you not to eat all the things you enjoy.

Not because I'm going to tell you to stop eating ice cream, chips, and that totally yummy frozen bread with the cheese baked in.

Nope!

You're going to hate me because once you try it, you're going to be telling yourself those things.

Hopefully, you'll listen to yourself, you'll listen to your body.

But first...

You have to be able to hear what your body is telling you. You'll learn how to listen.

Trust me, this is simple and requires only a small investment of time and willingness. I promise that the payoff is totally worth it. You'll shift life into the positive if you follow these simple steps.

Do I have your attention?

Good. *Read on...*

Wake up your awareness.

First...

Start by drinking at least 2-4 quarts of water a day. Yes! This can sound like a lot and yes, your whole body will thank you for doing it!

Next...

All too often we grab food on the run or eat without any attention to what we are actually consuming. We *all* do it. The key is to do it less often. The best way to become aware is through the following exercise.

Power-tip: Do it once with full attention and you'll prob-ably never look back.

The Practice:

Materials: one piece of a fruit or a nut you really like + one piece of your fave "go-to" snack whether it's salty or sweet + notepad + timer

Set aside twenty uninterrupted minutes. Lock the door, put the cat out, make someone else cook dinner or go for takeout. Grab your four items, sit down and take one of the "snack treats." Only one! If it's a tortilla chip then only one, same goes for any candy bar, etc... then *read* through, then practice once.

1. Unwrap the "snack item."

2. Hold in your hand and close your eyes.

3. Smell the item for 60 seconds.

4. Write down any aroma you noticed.

5. Note anything the flavor reminded you of (this might be a time, event, or place).

6. Take a <u>small</u> bite—do not chew or swallow just yet.

7. Let the bite sit on your tongue for 60 seconds.

8. Write what you notice, what are the sensations and flavors in your mouth? What other memories pop up?

9. Chew slowly for 30 seconds, try not to swallow.

10. What do you taste now and what's the texture? Pleasant, surprising, unpleasant; what's there that you didn't notice earlier?

11. Swallow or spit out, your choice.

Now go back and <u>do</u> the practice. Use your timer and do not rush. Complete any notes about what you experienced. Pay attention to memories if they came up. No need to judge them, simply note what they were and keep going.

Repeat the ten steps with a single bite of fruit or nut. This might be a single bite of apple or a single walnut or berry. Whichever you chose, a single bite is all you'll need.

What did you discover in comparison to the snack food? Which are you more likely to want in the future? Anything else you noticed? How does this new awareness shift what you choose to eat from now on?

Knowledge is Power.

Now that you've experienced really tasting your food, you can more easily change your eating habits. All the things you've read about how to eat more healthily hold true. It's a matter of adding them into your life in stages so you don't feel overwhelmed. Feel free to pick and choose from the list below. Do what suits you and try to add at least three of the Keys to Success listed below.

Healthy Eating Keys to Success:

♦ Shop at farmers' markets and local groceries whenever possible.

♦ Join a local CSA (Community Supported Agriculture farm).

♦ Shop the outer-most aisles of your supermarket (thanks to Michael Pollan for this one). The fresh items are always in the aisles around the perimeter. The closer to the center of the store you get, the more you're in the land of canned, frozen, and processed foods.

♦ Buy only as many fresh items you can consume in a week. It's fine to stock up on basics like beans, pasta, etc... But when the lettuce and greens wilt– you aren't gonna wanna eat 'em.

♦ Buy one cookbook you really like. Cook your way through it. By the time you finish, you'll be able to make almost everything you want from what you've learned. Better still, you'll be able to "wing it", impress your friends and family and have dishes turn out better than you expect most of the time.

♦ Forgive yourself any mistakes or over/undercooked dishes and the experiments gone wrong. For Pete's sake! That's why takeout is around.

♦ Eat a little slower than you're used to. Let yourself truly enjoy what you eat.

- Don't do other things while you eat. This includes reading, watching TV, checking your e-mails, or social media. Savor what you eat by paying attention.

- Start having seconds! <u>This means cutting your portions in half</u>. Eat the first half, wait for 20 minutes, then if you're still hungry, eat the second portion. Don't cheat on the time. It's a well-documented fact that it takes 20 minutes for your stomach to tell your brain that it's had enough.

Tips

- *We all make mistakes when cooking. I've been cooking for decades and 98% of the time it all tastes great, but when I mess up... I really mess up! Don't sweat it. Messed up a dish? Toss it, get takeout and try again another day.*

- *See additional sections on cooking for more help with building up your pantry.*

Cooking: General Stuff

You've got to eat.

You could spend all your money going out or ordering in, but even that gets old pretty quickly.

Plus, it's not the healthiest for your body or bank account.

If you already know how to cook some things, BRAVO!

If not, *don't panic or skip to the essay on "Nothing to Cook"*... I got you covered.

(And these days you have more resources than you can shake a cat at... provided it's not too large a cat.)

Cooking for one person is simple. Cooking for two or three is fun and cooking for more allows you to turn it into a dinner or potluck party. Everyone contributes and the fun increases exponentially.

The down-n-dirty truth is that cooking even simple things, (and I don't mean opening a packet of ramen), is something that will feed your body, feed your soul, win you friends, find you love, and generally make you feel better. You can even "revenge cook" which, truth be told, I do when I'm feeling particularly pissed off. I bake something extravagant, usually involving chocolate, nuts, caramel, and often all three, and then I give whatever fab-U-lous delight I've created to my neighbors. By the time I'm finished baking I feel less annoyed and the smiles I've gotten help shift my crappy mood. Over the years, my quirky habit has even gotten me invited to a bunch of awesome parties where of course I bring lasagna just to be contrary.

If you know how to boil water, then you can make all kinds of pasta, rice, lentils, vegetables, eggs, etc. You can even get fancy and make things like Dal (East Indian lentils) or blanch a variety of veggies to create dishes that have lots of tasty nutrition and are cooked just enough to make them seem like you spent lots of time (think: blanched asparagus stalks with olive oil and lemon drizzled over them).

You don't have to get a cookbook—though once you start cooking you may find that owning a decent cookbook with basic info is a great help. You can find almost any recipe online. It's simplest to start with what's already in your house, then search for recipes using those ingredients.

Expand your skills by heading to the nearest farmer's market or grocery store to pick up a few fresh items that you've never tried. Go for the ones with weird colors or shapes. Look up a couple of recipes and try them out. As you expand your skill, you'll discover the dishes you adore making and you can tweak each recipe to suit your own taste. Artistry in the kitchen is what it's all about.

Trust me when I say that no matter whether you're cooking a simple dish for yourself or a few friends, or you go all out and spend the day creating a feast, *practice increases accomplishment*. Feeling accomplished leads to increased self-assurance and that, dear reader, is a very appealing trait. The more you willingly throw yourself into experimenting and playing, the more confidence and fun you exude.

Tips

♦ *Start with simple dishes. Once you master a few of those, expand your palate and skills by taking on more challenging recipes and flavor combinations.*

♦ *Keep in mind: no matter how long you've been cooking or what your level of expertise is, we all make things that straight into the bin from time to time! It happens—whether it's the eggplant that you seriously over-salted or the pasta you forgot you were cooking which turned to paste... toss 'em! Forget 'em! Never happened! Try again.*

♦ *When in doubt, make grilled peanut butter and banana sandwiches.*

♦ *My favorite basic cookbooks, after half a century of serious cooking: The Williams Sonoma Cookbook, The French Chef Volumes I and II, Vibrant India, and The New Joy of Cooking.*

Nothing to Cook?

Stop right there!

Unless you literally do not have a single thing in your fridge or pantry, then you *always* have something to cook. It may not be amazing, but you can amaze yourself and others by creating a tasty meal out of "nothingness."

Interested? Read on...

Let's look at what you *do* have on hand.

Got pasta, rice, quinoa, or anything like that? *Potatoes or carrots will do in a pinch.*

Olive or other oil or butter? Lemon? Salt & pepper? Excellent! You've got the makings of a simple entreè. Now dig around in your fridge or freezer.... you're looking for *any other kind* of vegetable at all.

No veggies? Don't worry, you can use nuts (unless of course, you're allergic) ...

Roughly chop, then sauté veggies in 1 to 2 tablespoons oil/butter. In a separate pot or pan, cook the pasta or other grain/starch. Toss veg and starch together in a big bowl. Squeeze two tablespoons lemon juice over it and add salt and pepper to taste. If you like cheese, sour cream, or plain yogurt and have it, toss some in, (skip adding the lemon juice if you do this). Got parsley, basil, or cilantro? Mince that up and toss it in as well. Dried herbs also work well.

Hint: Choose one herb, not several for better flavor. Oregano, sage, marjoram, and some red pepper flakes can spark up a simple one-dish meal.

Another trick is to add a handful of toasted nuts. Every cuisine in the world has recipes for vegetables and meats which include nuts. Everything from pistachios and walnuts to peanuts (AKA: groundnuts) and almonds, all add protein and a certain richness to the taste of a dish. Like herbs, add one kind of nuts to a dish, not several.

The basic template is:

One starch (grain, potato, pasta...)

One to three different vegetables (or one handful of one type of nut)

One herb

One spice

Olive or other vegetable oil, ghee, or butter

Salt and pepper to taste

Optional:
Dairy or nut milk/sour cream, yogurt or cheese, peanut or nut butter.

One of the most useful side-effects of cooking with what you already have is that it can force you to explore new combinations of textures and flavors that you mightn't have tried. Often you'll come up with something better than expected.

Tips

♦ *Buy a couple of "exotic" cookbooks to spark ideas for different flavor combinations. My current faves include recipes from Georgia (the country), India, Morocco, and Israel.*

♦ *You don't need to have all the new spices or ingredients for a recipe to make something taste new and wonderful. Look at the qualities of the spices and ingredients; what are they achieving in the recipe? Each ingredient adds something specific, either bitter, sweet, smooth, creamy, salty, fiery, or tart. If you don't have a named ingredient, what do you have that would probably achieve a similar effect in the dish?*

♦ *Never add salt to the water you cook your pasta in—it toughens the pasta.*

Pantry

You need a pantry. Pantries save you money.
Here are the basics of what should be in your pantry:

- A few spices and herbs that you're familiar with and can name off the top of your head.

- A couple of exotic spices that you use occasionally for special dishes and may not yet, or ever be able to pronounce properly.

- One pound of each: staples that you eat like rice, lentils, beans

- Half a pound of each: dried fruits like raisins, cherries, dates, etc...

- A quarter pound of nuts in glass jars <u>kept in the fridge</u> to avoid them turning rancid.

- Four to five cans of soup

- Food storage bags and some glass or BPA-free containers

- Parchment paper for baking (also used for storing cheese in the fridge so it doesn't get slimy or mold too quickly).

- Glass containers for food storage

- One to three cans each of miscellaneous items like coconut milk, nut butters, simmering sauces, etc...

- One extra container each of whatever cooking oils you use.

- Some baking essentials (if you bake at all): flour, baking powder, pancake mix, baking soda, honey or other sweeteners, yeast, cornstarch, cocoa, and any special baking items you use often.

- If you consume alcohol then have a couple bottles of decent red and white wine, and/or beer/cider on hand.

Keeping a decent pantry means you can invite people over to share meals and you'll always be able to make something enjoyable. One of the great delights in life is a spur-of-the-moment invitation where you and your friends cobble together a meal from whatever's at hand. If you have a well-stocked pantry, these meals can feel like feasts for the soul!

Tips

- *Store nuts in glass containers and ideally somewhere cold or they'll go rancid. Most nuts stored at room temperature will stay fresh-ish for up to three months and refrigerated will remain fresh for up to a year. Pine nuts, Pistachios, and more oily nuts have much shorter shelf lives, like one to two months tops.*

♦ *Soups can often be used as simmering sauces, form the base for a stew, or be eaten "as is"—so they do triple-duty.*

♦ *Keeping the raw ingredients and learning how to cook basic things will also save you a whole heck of a lot of money and you'll feel more accomplished when you serve things you've made yourself, even if it's only you eating them.*

SECTION THREE

Name Change

As I write this, I'm preparing for an enormous change in my life. Not marriage (BTDT)... Not another move—though I'm pretty certain I'll be adventuring and exploring again at some point.

No, this time it's a step that feels even bigger to me... I'm changing my name.

Let me roll it back for a sec 'cause I know that might not sound like such a big thing.

What's the big deal? After all, people change their names all the frikken' time!

I'm with you on all that! AND...

My mind is warring with itself over this (and frankly, neither side is happy about the dispute).

Because, why...?

Because my mother changed her name several times

before I was 40, once forgetting to tell me until I walked into her classroom to surprise her and was confused to hear students asking for Leah when I knew her as Phaedra.

Because I follow a spiritual path and a new name was given to me at a moment marking my having reached an indeterminate (at least to me) level of devotion and awareness.

Because, generally... I like my name (Amy); it's short, and easy to spell, pronounce and sign in most languages.

Because it's hard for me to describe just why a new name feels exactly right.

And lastly, I'm nervous about how it will go over with people who've known me for less than a year or for more than 20.

Name changes are fraught with meaning. They signify all sorts of things like status, personality, desires, attitudes, accomplishments, etc... A name-change is wrapped, like ground pistachios, within layers of filo-thin and honeyed meaning. For example, when I got married, I briefly contemplated taking my husband's name to signify my new status as a "married woman." In the end, I decided not to, because at that point we were planning on having kids and I wanted them to have my surname along with his. Though to be honest, saddling a kid with a last name like Fishkin-Kosh, Kosh-Fishkin, or worse yet a hybrid like Fishkoshkin, would've been just plain cruel.

I did toy with various names growing up. In third grade, I insisted on being called Christopher and had several disagreements with my teacher who refused to call me "by a boy's name", *hello 1972!* My argument about why it shouldn't matter what name I wanted to be called notwithstanding, I felt entirely too satisfied when I brought in a copy of the *TV Guide* to show her the female actress on TV named Christopher.

I also went through an ill-considered spelling change in

fifth or sixth grade when I was attending public school in Philadelphia. It was all the fashion for "Amys" to go by "Aimee." An entirely unnecessary and complicated spelling. To be fair, the mid-'70s was also when we roped oversized Bonnie Bell Lipsmacker™ Lipgloss in peach or watermelon round our necks and Love's BabySoft™ was the scent of the year. Both also quite ill-advised. I transferred to an Ethical Society school the next year, dropped the "Aimee," and felt more myself again.

My newest Self feels different enough from who I've been that I hardly recognize "Me." We humans constantly change. Sometimes we make small adjustments—other times the shifts are gigantic. Sometimes we wind up BE-ing in ways that feel so sharply divergent we have to work hard to remember that once-upon-a-time we existed differently.

My journey has often been one of transformations wrapped in gossamer tangles and ribbons of discovery. Moving back to Rome, Italy, to study photography at age 23, I came home to myself, and to a city I loved. I was confident and relaxed from the moment I stepped from the metal gangway onto the sleet-encrusted January tarmac. My very American soon-to-be-pensione-mate was next to me. I led us through the maze of Italian corridors and checkpoints, customs tables, and questioners stamping passports. With each step, I recovered someone I'd left behind a decade earlier and had forgotten until reunited on that singular wintry day.

When I married at 44, I intentionally tried to BE different in the world. I was living in two semi-synced phases. Everything was new and yet not. I'd given up teaching photography, moved to a small New York town, and began my life as a "married New Yorker." I was an introvert who became known for monthly pot-luck and cocktail parties. The new me finally had the puppy I'd dreamt of raising. She was also a useful distraction when the despondency of not finding work enveloped me. The "old me" gardened, repaired dryers and furnaces, re-insulated and painted rooms, cleaned, organized, cooked, picked up work teaching yoga, and befriended the studio owners. On one level I had "succeeded"—I was, after all, married to a great guy, whom I genuinely liked and who would make a great father and husband. On another, I was 90% unemployed, feeling lost, unsure, and a complete failure. The two "mes" pulled and pushed. I felt like a wool sock dragged from the washer, stuck, and slowly elongating into shapelessness.

Now, I find myself unfolding into yet another version, from Amy to Amrita. I feel less like the 2.0 of an old self and more as though I'm being reborn. The process is slow. Steadily moving me to a life less-imagined than ever before.

We commonly assume each day will be much like the previous one. It's easy to see life as a river flowing steadily onward. We imagine we see far enough ahead that we can account for boulders or areas of rough water. Turning to look, we congratulate ourselves for having survived waterfalls or uprooted trees. The starting moments of our journey fade as the veil of time unfurls behind us.

My new name, Amrita Rose, arrived without hullabaloo or preamble, rather like someone had plunked it on my doorstep to be brought in with the post. It peered around the corners for a while before fully showing itself. Hesitant and excited, a small child visiting a county fair for the first time, wide-eyed at the colorful sights and clanging music. The name stuck around and began popping up at odd moments; in the shower, whilst walking my dog, poking my bicep as I sat writing, testing me for readiness. My coffee cup paused mid-sip one morning, I sat down to investigate this name in earnest.

The name has a nice sound. Familiar in some way, as though meeting a long-lost cousin with shared interests. It holds within its six letters apt descriptors for who I am and who I'm becoming. Most importantly, it feels like me with a capital "M" while the current three letters are more an old skin that tightens each morning I wake to it. This new name is shiny, sensitive as a snake newly shed of the last season.

The feeling of coming home to this name is what feels most important. I've found myself whispering it upon waking as though my body is moving me towards this new way of BE-ing, my mind following along. Like wading into the ocean from the shore, it's a gradual process of disintegration, rather than diving off the pier into the deep. I am BE-coming and becoming and becoming as wave upon wave sweeps me into this new sea of life.

You don't have to change your name to become new. You can grow yourself in directions you haven't yet imagined. You can expand your thinking, change your behavior and create a new outlook, though we don't usually shed our skin to demonstrate the differences.

New glasses, new hairstyle or color, new clothes and style of dress; all these are the ways you can demonstrate change. Be bold when you want the world to take notice. When you announce your changes "out loud" you invite comments, questions, and ultimately support for who you are and are becoming.

Don't Trash Yourself

Critical Voice or the Gremlin:

This is the voice (or voices) that arrive when you're getting ready to take a big leap towards your dreams and passions.

Think about the last time you went on a diet or planned to exercise every morning for 30 minutes—what happened? Often when we begin moving towards goals or passions, something gets in the way and says, *Really, do you really want to do that now?* Maybe you've been thinking about quitting your job or leaving a relationship—but all the seemingly logical reasons come rushing in to say why you shouldn't—this is Critical Voice (AKA: the Gremlin). It's the voice of self-sabotage that limit us and keep us in the life we have instead of the life we really want.

Critical voice fights to preserve the status quo. It chants a variety of messages to undermine you such as *It will never work out, you're not good enough, you don't know how to do that, why try?* critical voice throws every reason at you why *not* to take the risks that can lead to positive change. Critical voice doesn't like change and hates being ignored.

Risky Business

Following our critical voice can be a very risky business. It often doesn't feel like a risk, but you're trading the risks you know and *may be ignoring*, for ones you have not yet taken. The unknown risks always <u>feel</u> bigger and more dangerous.

Who Invited Critical Voice/Gremlin in?

You did. Yup. And you were probably too young to know you were doing it. Your C.V. or Gremlin is the voice of old teachers, parents, team coaches, bosses, community, and culture—anyone or any group who had an influence on you when you were young.

C.V. is usually the voice of people who wanted to keep you safe and out of harm's way. They meant well. As adults, we simply forget to let go of those early messages and choose our own adult ones. critical voice becomes internalized and we forget about it—we simply don't notice it any longer, letting it rule our lives and limit us following our dreams.

Not sure if you have a critical voice?

Want to hear your own critical voice? Take a minute right now to imagine quitting your job today or doing the one thing that you know in your heart would make you truly happy. What's the first argument that comes up against making that move? There's your internal stopper of a critical voice right there.

What are some of the phrases in your mind right now?

Now, think for a minute... is that *really* your voice saying that? Or is it the echo of a voice from your past? Critical voice always tries to tie us to the past—to past behaviors, past fears, or past events or people from childhood.

Raise Your Voice

Usually, the loudest voices are the ones that win. Our internal messages elbow each other for attention. We can be fooled into thinking they're our own voices because they seem rational, thoughtful, and familiar. But take a closer look and often we find that they're someone else's voice—one that we've internalized and given power to.

Raise your own voice by becoming aware of the internalized ones. Listen hard when doubt, fear, or "logical hesitation" come up, then take positive action. Write in a journal, talk out loud, find some way to have your say, and set the negative voice straight. *I often take myself on a long walk, arguing, out loud, each side until I see more clearly the old thoughts holding me back. The upside of arguing out loud in the woods is that rabbits and birds rarely seem to mind the ruckus.*

Risk and Critical Voice:

Critical voice is useful, so long as it doesn't run your life without you knowing it. Your C.V. can help you pause to consider possible risks. But if you're unaware, it can also keep you from creating what you desire most in your life. Critical voice can stop you living a life that feels amazing and unstoppable.

Make a Choice:

Once you become aware of your critical voice, you get to decide whether it's helping or hindering. You **always** have a choice whether to follow it and *stay in the same place you are now* or to raise your own voice, follow your heart and move to create the life you truly desire.

Your critical voice is the biggest, scariest monster you'll ever face. C.V. dredges up massive doubt, all the "what if's," and all your deepest fears. If you're really following your heart, I guarantee that critical voice will bring in the most powerful arguments to scare you off and talk you back into Option B. *You know Option B*—it's the safer, more reliable but "not-really-what-I-want" option.

Face your fears and become aware of how this negative or "safe" messaging holds you back. It can be scary and hard and super frustrating. *But just because something is scary and hard, doesn't mean you shouldn't do it!*

Hard Work Pays Off

Allow time to build your awareness of why you make a particular choice. Pay attention to how that choice affects you now and how it may shape the rest of your life.

Take a reality check: *Is what I have now what I want in five or 10 years? Would I be content if nothing changed?*

If you desire something to be different, then you need to take steps to create what you want. *Make a choice based on where you want to be*, not where you are right now. Trust that *you* know what's best for yourself now that you are an adult.

You always have some choice. Choose actions that move you toward your goals and passions. Choose to move into your best future, not remain stuck in past behaviors. You *always* have a choice, so what do you choose for yourself?

Allow Surprises

When's the last time you were surprised?

I mean well and truly surprised by something or someone?

We were all great at being surprised when we were kids—it was easier back then because so much in life was new. New things triggered our innate curiosity. But now? Most of us seem to have decided that it's not cool to be surprised so we stopped allowing or inviting curiosity into our lives.

Here's the thing about dialing down your ability to be surprised; when you scale that back, you limit your ability to feel joy and bliss along with lowering your capacity to see what's really going on in life. Inhibit your curiosity and you disallow many of the options, choices, and perspectives, along with all the emotions which enhance life.

One of the most valuable choices you can make is to elevate your curiosity. Not sure how to begin? Read on for some ways to get your curiosity tuned in and turned up and you'll notice more enjoyable surprises and enjoy being surprised more often.

Be willing to be surprised in life.
Think like a five-year old and don't lose your sense of wonder and amazement at the world.

Quick Start Curiosity

Each of these takes about three minutes. Go longer if you find one you enjoy.

Option 1

♦ Start first thing in the morning. Sit on the edge of the bed, close your eyes and take three easy exhales. Imagine your day is a huge whiteboard and you're erasing everything on it. Whether it's the list of things for the day, the anticipation of a meeting, or something you need to remember to do—wipe it away. Now imagine wiping away anything left from yesterday and any days before that. Erase all the thoughts and memories from the past four to five days. Wipe out any and all "should have," "need to," and "why didn't I...?" Let yourself "see" a perfectly clean board in your mind. It's your clean slate for the day. Notice if any thoughts come in; if so, erase them gently.

Now visualize one thing that you'll take with you for the day. Maybe it's a feeling of confidence, delight, or ease. You could visualize feeling a sense of purpose or accomplishment. Next, grab a piece of paper and write the three most important tasks for the day (no more than three). Use these tasks to focus your actions—tackle each one in turn. When they're complete, add the next three. At the end of the day, you can choose to transfer any incomplete tasks to the next day—or start fresh again.

Option 2

♦ No matter where you are in your day, focus on the next physical action you need to take (writing a note, reading a draft, making a call, or scheduling an appointment). Whatever it is, as you move into action allow yourself to do it as though for the very first time. Let yourself explore how it feels. Notice differences in texture, weight, or the physical movement you're performing. Once you've completed that task, bring the same curiosity and wonder to each new action you take.

Option 3

♦ At the end of the day, imagine shedding everything that occurred the same way you remove your coat or shoes. Let your mind wander back to one thing in your day that surprised you. Try not to name it "good" or "bad." Instead, explore what happened and what about it surprised you. Were you expecting something different? Was it something you desired or something you'd rather not deal with? Let your curiosity roam and notice what thoughts come up. Make a quick note of whatever thoughts arise and then let the exercise go (I like burning the paper as a way to really let this shit go). Do this each evening. At the end of the week make a quick review of what you notice as you continue this awareness practice.

Why is being curious and surprised a good thing?

There are two important benefits to increasing the amount of curiosity and surprise we experience each day.

The more we allow surprise the less uncomfortable we feel when it pops up. What happens is called hedonic adaptation. As we increase awareness of something, we acclimate to it and it stops feeling new. The more we practice awareness, the more we build in a pause or break between whatever triggered our reaction and what response we have to it. Being aware of the surprise and noting the action we choose to take increases our ability to choose smarter actions and see more options in the heat of the moment. It allows us to thoughtfully respond rather than unthinkingly react.

Building a habit of being curious invites multiple solutions to every situation. By creating a pause between the event and the response, we are more capable of taking considered action that moves us towards our desired outcome. In plain speak— we get better at making bad situations better rather than worse when we stop, breath, and act with intention. Practicing this we make better choices, see more options, and are able to stay on course and feel happy, rather than be derailed or feel the day ruined when something surprising occurs.

Tips

♦ *Practice makes perfect! Creating that momentary pause before you take action is a skill. The more you practice the better you get at it.*

♦ *Be patient with yourself. Learning any new thing takes time and repetition. You aren't going to master the "pause" overnight and that's okay. You don't need to.*

Being Generous is Selfish

Being generous, truly generous is the most selfish thing you can do.

Wait... What?

You might have been taught that being generous is the "right" thing to do, or the kind thing. As little kids, we're taught to share our toys. Grow up in a city and you were likely taught to share your space on the bus or train. We share food with those we love and those we are trying to get to love us. Sometimes we share money, belongings, beliefs, or dreams with others, but sharing and being generous aren't really about the other person.

Being generous has profound positive effects that can make "giving" even more beneficial than receiving.

Positive Psychology has been tracking the data for years and the numbers show that when you fill someone else's "kindness bucket" by being generous to them, you're filling your own bucket-o-love at the same time.

♦ People who are generous report greater satisfaction in all areas of their lives.

♦ They have more friends and more friends who are willing to do them favors, than people who are not generous.

♦ Generosity builds stronger relationships across the board. Whether you're being generous to friends or people you simply come into contact with, you'll form stronger bonds with everyone you relate to.

♦ Being generous results in more satisfaction at work, no matter what your work is. This is directly related to the next point which is that people who are generous have a more positive outlook on life in general.

♦ Whether you're a pessimist, optimist, optimalist, or realist, being more generous will increase your experience of positive feeling and mindset.

♦ Generosity increases physical and mental health. Highly generous people were less likely to feel negative emotions like anxiety, depression, apathy, or hopelessness. Acting from generosity also lowers the risk of dementia and improves chronic pain management.

♦ Increased satisfaction with what you have is a terrific side-effect of being generous. You'll save money and create a more sustainable financial future for yourself since you won't feel as much compulsion to go out and buy the next "shiny thing."

♦ Generous people feel better about themselves; they have markedly higher self-esteem.

◆ Being generous reduces stress in the body. One study found that in many cases being generous reduced high blood pressure as much as medicine and exercise.

◆ As a cumulative effect of all these points, being generous can help extend your life expectancy.

All this boils down to meaning that you get far more out of being generous than you're likely to give, so do it! No excuses about how you don't have time, or how you have to wash your hair, your windows, or the cat. Stop procrastinating about what it might cost you in time, energy, or money. Those are stalling tactics and the more you let them stop you, the fewer benefits you'll reap.

The truth is that being generous is truly selfish.

At the end of the day, if you have been generous with others and *WITH YOURSELF,* you have helped create a better, nicer, kinder, more compassionate, and thoughtful and responsive world. Since you get to live in this world, that means you've been selfish by helping create it.

Stop and think for a moment about how it feels to give an unexpected surprise to someone else. Maybe it's buying the person behind you a coffee. Maybe you wave that other car into your parking spot on shopping day when it's super-crowded. Each time you open a door for someone else, smile or wave hello as you pass on the street or the trail, you'll feel a little lightness of heart. When you give yourself a break, go for a quick walk, or take a few moments to gaze at the sky you give yourself a mental boost and some self-compassion. The joy you feel, the tingling that makes you smile when you see how much a small act of generosity brightens someone's day, simultaneously fills your bucket-o-joy.

Get your imagination going and make a list. Do it now! Don't think too much! List ten simple ways you could be generous with someone today. Think of physical actions that take less than two minutes and cost you less than $2 (like smiling and holding the door as you walk into your fave morning coffee shop).

Got it? Great!

Now list 10 things you could do to be generous with yourself today. *Again, DO NOT overthink this stuff!*

List 10 ways you could be more compassionate, or loving to yourself. How can you be a smidge more patient or forgiving of the fact that you're human? What quick actions would make you smile if someone else did them for you out of the blue? What might you do or say to your partner, child, friend, family member, or co-worker to cheer them up? Next, do a couple of those for yourself as well.

Small acts of generosity matter, often more than big ones. Why? Because small acts don't feel like they have a "price tag" attached. Small acts of random generosity are done purely for the moment. They don't feel like someone is looking for a thank you. Small acts don't require anything from the recipient. Maybe the person you buy coffee for thanks you... maybe you do it anonymously, either way, you reap the benefits.

Every small and larger kindness goes straight to your own heart and lifts you up. Being generous can cheer you on a crappy day. It can help alleviate "the blues" by reconnecting you to your own ability to be appreciated and create joy in the world.

So go on! Be selfish and be generous!

Tips

- *Want a great visual for being generous? Imagine you're at the beach and you have a pail in each hand; one is yours; the other is for someone else. Every time you do something generous, both pails get seashells. Do something for someone else gets them two shells and you one. Being generous with yourself gets each pail one seashell. If you're being generous to someone, including yourself, then everyone benefits.*

- *You'll have more fun and reap more benefit if you make generosity to others a daily habit. Practice every day for 21 days to build your new habit.*

- *Being generous to yourself falls under the umbrella of self-care and self-worth. That's a whole other can of sardines that we'll tackle in a separate section. For now, trust me when I say that the most important person to be generous with is yourself!*

Be Honest with Yourself

I have a friend who recently lamented that women keep leaving him. He was truly puzzled by this. I could also see why someone just meeting him would also be surprised. He's a smart, sexy, outdoorsy guy who is sweet and kind and thoughtful. He went on to say that he'd had a few longer-term relationships but each and every one of these women had either walked away or departed with harsh words that left him reeling and bewildered. He was asking me what he might be doing or not doing to bring this misery into his life. He knew there must be *something* but he couldn't see it for himself. It was something that bugged him enough that he started asking questions about it.

Being friends with a life coach does have its benefits...

What was going on? This guy has the external package that makes women run toward him. Unfortunately, they were running away almost as quickly, and it was tearing his heart into teeny, tiny shreds. He had started to think he'd never find true love.

So what exactly was happening here?

Why would women walk away from all that attractiveness?

Well... He's wearing plaid and doesn't know it.

What?

The guy wears a plaid shirt? What's wrong with that?

It's a suit.

A whole goddamned plaid *suit*.

And it's invisible.

We all have plaid suits of one kind or another. They're the *stories* we tell ourselves about who we are. They're our patterns of behavior, and habits. Aaaand... Surprise! A lot of the time we don't know we've shrugged them on. In fact, we have often completely forgotten that we've got a choice every day whether to wear plaid or grab our fave pair of jeans.

A plaid suit can look like the reason someone never asked for what they want in life. It can keep people stuck in jobs they hate because they feel like they "should" be working there. It can drag our hearts into solitude or constant frustration. Our plaid suits keep us stuck in the past—in stories of who or what we *think* we are.

A plaid suit is the pattern that we haven't looked at in our lives, the one that colors everything we do and say, that filters how we see everything everyone else does as well.

So what the hell do we do about our own plaid suit? *Because, you know, it's clashing all over the place with everyone else's plaid suit.*

It's pretty simple.

We have to be willing to admit that we've each got a story that we keep repeating to ourselves about ourselves, about other people, about the world. We always have a choice to change our story and trust me, we *all* have some sort of story... We have to find our story, hold it at arm's length and notice where it's ripped, frayed, outdated or simply no longer fits who we are.

Not sure what yours is? Try this five-minute practice and I bet your story shows up loudly declaring itself:

- ◆ Grab a pen, paper, and a timer.

- ◆ Set the timer for two minutes.

- ◆ Now pick a topic—life, work, relationship, or other topic of your choice.

- ◆ Start the timer and, for two minutes, list as much as you can about your topic.

- ◆ Try to list everything you can think of as it comes to mind.

- ◆ Write for the whole two minutes without thinking too much

- ◆ Turn your paper over, stand up and stretch or look out the window for a minute, or two, or ten.

Now come back, read through your list, and notice what items could fall under the heading of persistent/pervasive thinking. Persistent/pervasive thinking is the "always" or "all" category. For example, if I listed out things that I've heard my friend in his plaid suit complain about, it'd be that women "always" leave him, that people are "always" selfish, (and the killer) "I'm (always) shy."

So what items on your list have that persistent or pervasive quality?

Give those babies a check-mark ✔

Now check your story—

For each checked item, can you think of one example

where that isn't true? Maybe you wrote that "people are selfish." What about Gandhi? There's the example of non-truth (though it could be argued that Gandhi was the ultimate selfish person by desiring a world free of repression).

Review your list, look for examples that break the persistent thought pattern. You'll start to see a new pattern emerge. There's the story you can now choose to tell yourself. Ask yourself... "What will change if I'm willing to ditch the old and live into the new?"

You have an opportunity to write a new story. Go ahead, give it a shot.

What new truth can you find in your life when you shrug outta that plaid suit?

The truth is that we create the stories of our lives and then forget that we told tall tales. We wear the old patterns out of habit because we never look in the closet and see that right there, to the left of that old plaid suit... is an awesome pair of jeans.

And that old plaid suit?

Burn it!

You ARE Creative

Yesterday a friend asked me to write about an eggplant. We'd been sitting outside at 7:15 am at our "coldest-mornings-coffee-spot" (the one with the outdoor fire-pit) and talking about colors, vegetables, food, and writing. I suspect he meant it as a joke, since he never imagined I'd actually want to write about this monolithic fruit which most people see as a vegetable

The moment he tossed the topic out I thought of current texting habits and how the eggplant has taken on a wholly different meaning within the world of texting and dating. The humble eggplant has in fact become a staple of sexual innuendo in such variety that it has seasoned the pot of creativity simply by being itself.

Voluptuous as the shape is, the deep purple color adds to the sensual quality and the current generation has picked up on what thousands of cooks have known for hundreds of years—that the humble eggplant is, beyond being a sexy emoji, the convergence between sensuality and creativity.

Creative how?

One of the easiest ways to tap into our own oft-hidden creativity is through our physical senses. Often we need to be provoked by something that comes to us through touch, taste, sight, hearing, or smell. Once we get a whiff or a glance of something that intrigues or frightens us, our creativity and imagination are off and running. The key is to harvest the fruits of the provocation, take them, and grow them into something bigger, more interesting, and more exciting than that of the root idea which spurred us in the first place (all puns intended).

"Oh, but I'm not creative at all!"

That's a comment I hear all the time and I can tell you right now that if you're a living human on this planet, then you have already proven that you're creative.

Doubt me? Let's take a minute for a reality check.

Have you ever:

—Cooked a meal of any kind without reading a recipe?

—Gotten dressed without looking at a picture of what to wear?

—Solved a problem at work or at home?

—Moved from one home to another and packed/ unpacked by yourself?

—Worked at a new job?

—Taught someone else to do something new to them?

If you answered yes to any one of these then you have been creative.

"Oh, well... I thought you meant could I make art or music or something like that. That's what I think being creative really is!"

Bosh and Balderdash! Take your head out of your arse and stop limiting your idea of creativity.

Whenever we do something new we have to be creative. We are required under the circumstances to recombine knowledge in new ways to meet whatever new challenge we find ourselves faced with.

Creativity is not in producing artwork, it's in the creative problem-solving that goes on at the inception of an idea.

Let's drag that eggplant back in for a moment. What can we do with this odd and beautiful fruit?

When presented with an eggplant, we can cook it. Use it as a model for any number of drawings. Practice mixing paint to get just the right shade of aubergine. Carve it, drop it from tall buildings, use it as a blimp in a diorama (do kids even make those anymore?). Core and seed it to grow next year's eggplant crop. We can even use it as a prompt for writing about creativity and/or sex.

Creativity, much like eggplants and sex, exists even when we're not thinking about it. By limiting what we call "being creative", (much like limiting "being sexy"), we limit ourselves in ways that don't serve us. When we tell ourselves that we aren't creative or sexy, we negate all the truly creatively sexy and sexily creative things we do every day.

When you flip the script and start owning up to your own creative and sexy abilities they, like well-watered eggplants, will grow. Give yourself permission to think creatively and you'll increase your creative output along with building confidence in your own abilities.

By acknowledging your own inherently human creativity, (and sexiness) you'll build those muscles, (pun intended again). As we all know, the more we practice doing anything, the better we get at doing it.

So... go out there, give yourself permission to be the authentically whole and holistic human that you are. Allow yourself to practice being and doing "Creative"! More important, acknowledge your creativity as it shows up. Invite it for tea, allow it to sit alongside you at work, and when that next big problem rolls in you'll already have a terrific new friend to help you solve the problem.

Tips

♦ *Don't limit yourself to playing with eggplants. Think of one object you come into contact with each day and stop to ask yourself, "How many things can I do with this?" For example, if I handed you a brick and asked you to write down as many things you can think of to do with it, how many could you come up with in two minutes?*

♦ *Being creative is not about being artistic! Creating art, music, dance, writing, architecture, or any number of other "artistic products" is often something that people have spent years learning and practicing how to do. The creativity comes not in producing the artwork, it comes in the creative problem-solving that goes on at the inception of an idea.*

Response-Ability

"*Who's* responsible *for this?*"

That's the common way to ask, "Who can I blame for this?"

Who's responsible for this?

Is really a question of understanding our own ability to respond—to anything and everything—all the time.

The truth is we don't have a choice about being able to respond. We do it without thinking. Breathing is a response to our need for oxygen. Pain is a response that keeps us from doing a whole lot of stupid stuff that could kill us, like cutting off an ear or nose for fashion. Flinching or yelling when surprised is a response that's also linked to keeping us alive and on the planet. Laughing is our response to what feels good. Laughing in turn triggers a deeper response that bathes our insides with happy-making chemistry so we do our best to keep responding in a way that builds more and more good feeling.

We respond 100% of the time, to everything and anything. Many of our responses are out of our conscious control, and often outside of our awareness.

Action is a whole different ballgame!

We <u>always</u> have a choice about which action to take based on a particular response. We can choose to reach out and move forward. We can just as easily choose to stay put or retreat. We choose whether we walk towards or away from something. We choose whether we say something and what words we spill out into the world.

The biggest problem we have is creating a pause between a response and our actions.

All too often we muddle response with taking action and think they're the same thing.

They aren't.

Your response to something—let's say, getting fired—and the actions you choose to take next are two steps in a process. The process can either walk you closer to something that feels good, or closer to something that feels icky, but the choice is always 100% yours.

The more space you create between a response and the action you choose to take, the better the outcome.

Why? Because humans want to be happy and alive and when you stop to notice what response you're having, you'll make choices for action that aim you more directly towards happiness and aliveness.

It's human nature.

The trouble starts when we respond to something and take action immediately and without thinking.

AKA: The "knee-jerk" response.

Taking action without thinking is what gets us humans into trouble. It leads to all sorts of things from bar fights and brawls, to arguments, altercations, divorces, and dumb-ass moves that take us further away from what we really want. Whatever we really want.

Being able to notice a response you're having better allows you to see what is causing the response in the first place.

"...watch your surroundings, rather than constantly reacting to them. Instead of your surroundings setting the tempo for you to dance to, by pausing, you can choose to set your own tempo where it makes sense. You don't respond to everything; only to the things that are right for you." ~Zat Rana, journalist

Whether it's a boss yelling, a teacher or coach telling us off, or a family member who rants and raves about something for the first or the thirteenth time, when we pay attention to our own response, we are more apt to take action that de-escalates the tension for everyone involved. This lowers stress and allows us to choose the best course of action. When we are under less stress, we make better, smarter, clearer choices than when we are in "survival mode."

So, the next time something winds you up, exhale 3 times, notice what your response is and think about the next best action you can take. It might be exhaling a few more times, it might be walking away, it might be laughing... you won't know what's possible until you try it.

Tips

- ♦ *If you're in a situation and notice that your heart rate has sped up, your breathing is shallow, you feel hot or are clenching your fists, then you're having an avoidance response. This is the time to take those three to five exhales and buy yourself time to calm down before you take any action at all.*

♦ *90% of the time the smartest thing you can do is nothing for 72 hours. Most ordinary and even many extraordinary situations either resolve themselves in 72 hours or will present you with new perspectives and options for solutions that you'll not see in the "heat of the moment."*

Relationships

First off, I'm not going to tell you how to have more sex, *though I think we should all have more, great sex.*

I'm also not going to tell you how to meet *The One* in 90 days, or seven weeks or even in a year, because I believe we can be the one for more than one person and there is more than one person who can be the great love in our life.

Finally, I'm not here to tell you how to run your team, organize your company or create a better connection with your supervisor or boss, *though all those will happen if you follow the steps below.*

What's on offer here is a gritty-nitty-let's-not-waste-time-get-right-to-it guide for creating better, deeper, more authentically satisfying relationships in every aspect of your life and doing it in the simplest, most effective way possible.

Sounds radical? Perfect!

We're going for radical change here.
Something totally new!
Let's-get-right-to-it-steps!

10 Ways to Create Satisfyingly Juicy Relationships:

1. Know Yourself, Know Your Core Values.
When you know who you are and what you stand for it's easier to show up audaciously in every relationship, whether with your girlfriend, boyfriend, boss, parent, or kids (AKA: any other being on the planet). Many of us grow into adulthood taking ourselves for granted because, well... we've been on the journey with ourselves and we know what happened along the way.

Knowing the events, seeing how we've been impacted by them is helpful, but it's not the same as understanding who we are and what drives our way of BE-ing in the world. Once we get clear on what BE-ing our SELF means, it's easy to see where we've fallen out of alignment.

"You do you, I'll do me." ~Sylvan, age 4

Your core values are what drive your actions. They're the ways you show up in the world, they define who you are and they can shove you around better than any after-school bully if you don't take some time to say hello and share your PBJ with them. At the back of this book, you'll find a list of core values to use for this practice.

Core values are the "non-negotiables." Often we're not conscious of them. Take a couple minutes and define your core values out loud by doing any or all of the following:

♦ Ask three people *who know you really well* for three adjectives they'd use to describe you.

♦ Think back on your life, what three adjectives would you use to describe yourself?

♦ Ask three people whom you met very recently what three adjectives they'd use to describe you.

♦ Add one more for good measure.

Now you have your top ten core values for your list. These are not aspirational values, they're who you already are BE-ing in the world. They're how you show up when you aren't thinking about it.

♦ Take all those words, write them down and notice how you're showing up in the world. Are you BE-ing courageous, active, thoughtful, persistent, inquisitive? Notice that for every adjective (core value) there is a shadow side and a light side; for example, "stubborn" is the flip side of "persistent" and "courageous" can be flipped to "foolhardy." It's all in how you put them into action.

♦ Order the words from juiciest (to you), to least powerful. What are your top three core values?

♦ Name your top three core values out loud. Write them on sticky notes, spread them around, remind yourself of them visually every day for 30 days. Live large with them.

♦ Know your top three core values so well that you can say them out loud, forwards and backwards. Embed them in your heart and embody them in your actions.

When you know where you're going, many roads will get you there.

When you know what's driving your actions, you're in charge of them. You can choose to elevate values that are lower down on your list. Notice which values you are bringing into play at this moment. How does that value help right now? Would a different value be more useful in the situation? Once you see which values you're leaning into, you can choose which ones to bring to the party.

2. To Thine Own Self Be True.

Shakespeare said it way before herds of psychologists echoed his words. Now that you're aware of your top ten core values you can use them to define the kind of life you want to live, one that is fully aligned with the values you named as being who you really are.

When what you say, do, think and feel are fully aligned, you'll live an unstoppable life. If you expend energy in different directions, it's almost impossible to reach your goals.

One of the simplest ways to align yourself is to write a personal manifesto.

Write Your Personal Manifesto:

Start with five minutes of writing. You can always write more if you want. What do you know is true and what do you believe in? You can start with: *"I believe in...," "I know this is true...," "I create... in the world."*

Take some time over several days or weeks to create your manifesto. Read it a couple times, refine it, and remember—this is a living document that can and should change as you grow. Revisit it once a year and update it to reflect who you are and who you want to grow yourself into. The more often you reflect on how you align to your manifesto, the more you'll find life becoming easier. When you expend your energy in one clear direction, you increase your awareness and are more able to seize opportunities as they come along.

PS: There is a full resource on writing your personal manifesto at the end of this book.

3. Isn't She Lovely, Isn't She Wonderful?

Stevie Wonder had a hit with this song in part because he reminded us all of how we feel when we first meet someone we like. Whether you're falling in love, just met a new bestie, or a new great boss or team—we all feel that deep satisfaction when we connect deeply with another person.

One way to keep relationships strong is to practice seeing each person you know as though you are meeting them for the first time. Whether you're in the middle of a project together at work, or sitting down to breakfast with your family or partner, imagine they are new to you. How do you greet them? How would you like to get to know them today?

There's a saying: *You can't go home again.* The people who raised us often have a hard time seeing us for the capable adults that we have become, and it's not only parents who do this. We all fall into the trap of thinking that we *know* someone (especially if we live with them). Changes in thinking and attitudes are incremental and easy to miss in ourselves, never mind tracking shifting beliefs in someone we live or work with daily.

Start each day with an attitude of gratitude for each person you connect with to invite freshness into the relationship. When we stop assuming we know how someone will react, we create a space for new thoughts, new behaviors to emerge. Simultaneously this allows us to check our reactions and chose actions that create positive growth rather than friction.

4. Do Something Different.

When you get yourself out there and do something new, you gain a whole slew of benefits (never mind no one really knows how big a slew is...). Doing something new expands your thinking and bumps you out of the furrow you're used to. You can meet new people and make new friends. When you test yourself and do something you've never done before you increase your resilience and self-confidence.

Take a few minutes to write out what a typical week looks like for you. Notice how often you're doing things that you've done a million times before—grocery shopping at the same places, going to the same parks or bike trails, taking the same way home from work, walking your dog along the same paths. Notice how often you're "ant-tracking" by taking the same routes or the same actions from memory.

Pick one thing to do differently this week. It can be small like trying a new way home from work or school. Maybe you check out a different part of town or bike instead of drive. Maybe it's bigger—you head to a new coffee shop and chat with someone you meet there, perhaps plan an outing to a new trail, town, or park. If you want to get really bold you could travel, bungee jump, or sky-dive.

Want to go really big? Change your thinking about something you think you know "for sure." Taking time to think in new ways can radically change your life. When you think "different" you also change the people around you and that's a "life-changer" for everyone!

5. Share a Project or Task with Someone.

Shared efforts deepen all kinds of relationships when we see them as building communication. Whether we share household chores or projects at work, we have opportunities to create bonds with others. Rather than the common "divide and conquer" method where we divvy-up tasks, invite a spirit of camaraderie by outlining the bigger picture first. Whether it's a family doing a weekly "house clean" or part of a team at work, when you begin by including others in the planning and the doing, you increase levels of thoughtfulness and companionship that deepen the connection with others.

Many hands make light the work,
many hearts lighten the soul.

6. Take Listening Walks.

Sounds funny, but all too often when we catch up with friends we're so excited about sharing our news that we don't really *listen* to the other person. The flip-side is that our friends, however dear to us, are doing the same thing, so no matter how many words are exchanged, there's often a deeper level of understanding and connection that goes missing.

Listening walks deepen our connection to others by inviting thoughtful attention and consideration of what the other person is saying. They create a space for us to be truly heard and that grounds us in our reality, whatever it may be. When we feel fully heard it translates to a feeling of belonging even if someone disagrees with us. Being heard is not the same as agreement, but it goes a long way towards understanding and acceptance of differences.

The next time you want to catch up with a friend, find a place to walk while you talk. Allow the other person to talk for half the distance while you simply listen carefully to whatever they have to say. Don't interrupt with questions, comments, or even the murmured "hmmm..." *Listen* to what happens as they unfold the story on their own. Listen for how they feel about what they relate to you, how do you notice they feel? At the end, ask whatever <u>single</u> question you really need to understand what they said and offer one or two short thoughtful observations (if asked). Take your time, then it's your turn to be heard.

Notice how it feels to have someone truly pay attention to you. How is it different to be fully heard and not questioned while you're unfolding your tale? Notice how your bond with this person has deepened as you both were able to *hear* more than just the words or just the situation being retold.

BONUS ROUND! Walk with someone you may be in disagreement with. Listen closely and without needing to respond while they lay out their thoughts. Then take your turn and notice as you talk how you may feel a shift in the emotions you're experiencing.

7. Give Your Self Time Off.

Regularly set aside time for yourself. Whether you take five minutes, an hour, or a day, we all need time to recharge, release, and reground ourselves. When you gift yourself regularly scheduled "time off" you provide time to integrate the unexpected and exciting events that happen in life. The more integrated you are, the more attention and thoughtful-ness you bring to your life and the more you increase your resilience.

You can carve out time for yourself by intentionally creating a pause between tasks, or between locations. You can choose to set aside a few hours one day a week to play, relax, or do whatever nourishes your body and your heart (soul). When you give yourself a gift of time, you're upgrading your entire life.

8. Just Do It!

The healthier your body, the better you feel. When we feel physically happy we are more empathic, compassionate, and kind. By exercising regularly in a ways you enjoy and eating healthily, you'll increase those attributes which build better relationships.

This doesn't mean go do your hardest workouts all the time, those are great for when you need to blow off steam, or if you're training for a competition. I'm talking about basic walks, running, dancing, biking, hiking, gym, sex, swimming... you get the picture. Nothin' too crazy, just enough to move your body in ways that feel good and leave you feeling relaxed.

(And yes... I did say sex.)

9. Send a Note of Thanks.

It used to be de rigueur to send a thank you note after attending a dinner, or to ring someone to show appreciation for a thoughtful act. These days that's not so much the case, which is sad because when we fill someone else's happiness pail, we fill our own. Studies in Positive Psychology demonstrate that when we express gratitude for a kindness, or appreciation for another, we increase our own feelings of happiness and inclusion.

Send a note of thanks or appreciation for someone once a month. Maybe it's for something they said or did, or simply something delightful you notice about them—whatever the topic, you can keep it short-n-sweet or wax poetic and go lengthy, your preference. By sharing, you spread that appreciation around and multiply it.

10. Practice Kindness and Wonder.

Small acts of kindness, surprise, and wonder can change your life in ways you can't imagine if you don't try them. Buy a coffee for the person next in line, pick up trash that you see on a walk, say hello with a smile, take on a task for someone else at home or work, or send a small and surprising gift to some "just because." All these are ways to deepen your relationships. Whether it brings a smile, a word of thanks, or makes the world prettier for others, you also benefit.

Appreciating others fills your happiness pail, as does practicing random acts of kindness and wonder. Those'll give you happiness spilling over the top. You'll find yourself feeling lighter every time you create a smile or lightness for others and that IS priceless.

Tips

- *There are whole books written for each of those topics and each can teach you something valuable if you read this and decide you want to dive deeper, hit up Google or your local bookseller for a list of books on anything I'll cover here— trust me, there are plenty of in-depth resources out there for you.*

- *Whether you walk in person or jump on a call for the conversation, walking is essential. We humans process information differently when we are moving than when we sit still. Movement increases our empathy and our ability to digest information more easily and quickly. I've noticed that by walking as we listen or share information, we tend to walk out the more volatile emotions and increase our own ability to shift from static to growth mindset and from anger to solutions.*

Build a Great Relationship with Yourself

In today's world, we don't often get the chance to learn this skill.

Being alone is too often associated with not having friends, or with being lonely.

It's neither of those.

Being alone leads you down a path of self-awareness and discovery. It means being *with* your self.

When you spend time with yourself, uninterrupted by anyone else, you get real clear, real fast, about what's genuinely important to you. And you know who else in the world takes the time to identify what is really important to them? Successful and happy people.

The happiest and most successful people on the planet have taken the time to get to know themselves. They've identified their likes and dislikes. They've clarified and defined their desires and goals. They know what drives them to action and what saps their energy and joy.

By knowing these things, you level up your life. When you can articulate what you want to create for yourself, you see the action steps needed to create it.

Radical idea: Being alone ultimately leads to more delight, more joy, and a greater sense of confidence and purpose.

When you practice being alone, you're taking time to befriend yourself.

Sitting by yourself on a sunny hillside for a couple hours, no book, no phone, just you and your "date"—i.e., your Self/Soul/Spirit.

This is when you really find out who the person called "Me" is.

What do you like? What pisses you off?

All the questions you would ask on a first, second, or fifth date... go on... ask 'em!

What's your favorite color, or flavor of ice cream? Was it always that?

What annoys you and do you catch yourself doing it to others?

Is what you have in life satisfying you, what would make it even better?

What makes you laugh on rainy days?

Would you give yourself permission to do it more often?

When you practice being alone, you create a deeper awareness of your core values, drives, and goals. Alone time helps you appreciate your accomplishments and take action towards goals you really, truly want. Goals that are fully aligned with what your heart yearns for, and with who you are in your most authentic moments.

Knowing yourself invites you to BE your most authentic.

"The longer I'm out in the wilderness, the quieter my mind gets. My DNA remembers living like this. It just feels right."
~ Callie Russell, Wilderness Skills Instructor

If you haven't spent much time alone, be patient.

Your *Self* is probably a little shy. You probably haven't invited your spirit or soul out in a long time and you may gasp at how spacious it feels to do so. With a little patience, you'll find that being alone is a pretty amazing way to spend an hour, a day, or longer (once you get the hang of it). With continued practice, you may even find yourself craving alone time!

Learning to be alone and knowing who you really are, without anyone else's ideas getting in the way, is a surefire way to creating lasting resilience, happiness, contentment and success in life.

Give it a try!

You've got absolutely nothing to lose and everything to gain.

Tips

Note: I use the terms Self, Soul, and Spirit interchangeably here. You can choose the term you like best or make up one for yourself.

♦ *Being alone and feeling lonely are not the same thing. Being alone is about allowing you to get to know your Self/Soul/ Spirit. Loneliness is an experience of feeling disconnected, while desiring connection with others.*

♦ *Take it slowly. If you aren't used to spending time alone, start by taking your Self on a date for a half-hour. Pack a picnic, bring a journal, go somewhere peaceful and quiet. Sit with your Self, take some notes about what you experience as you sit quietly. What comes up for you? What emotions or ideas pop into your mind as you spend time alone? Jot down any themes and then explore one of them.*

♦ *Be curious about ideas or emotions that arise. See where they lead without needing to arrive at any particular destination or answer. You're an explorer, not a conqueror.*

Romance

The other day my friend told me that the way she saved her romance with her boyfriend was to stop thinking about him as her boyfriend. We both inhaled looked at each other and shared one of those "A-HA!" moments...

Why?

Because most of the time, when we start thinking about our romantic relationships as being different or more special than any other relationship, we tend to screw them up with expectations and behaviors that would have imploded any other relationship within the first 24 hours.

Don't believe me? Try this quick test.

List five things you expect from your friends.

List five things you expect from your family.

List five things you expect from your romantic partner.

What differences do you see?

We often expect our romances to be perfect in one way or another and let me tell you, we humans are pretty darned short-tempered and snotty to people who aren't meeting our expectations. We're not mean like the nasty girl in high school, or the mean guy on the bus... until we are.

The funny thing is, most of the time we're unaware that we're holding our romantic partners to a whole different standard.

For example, you make a date to go run with a friend, and at the last minute, he texts to say he can't make it and he's sorry. Do you quiz him about why? Do you get mad and yell back at him? Or do you let it go and make a new plan for another time? Now imagine it's your partner who pulls the same thing... last-minute text canceling. Do you jump on the phone and start berating or do you let it go the same way you did for your friend? Be honest!

Maybe you're one of the few people who have already figured out that your romance is the same as every other relationship you have, but if you're still expecting your partner to be the be-all-and-end-all for you, listen up! *All relationships are the same in several ways, even work relationships. This is not to say that you want to have identical expectations for all your relationships. What you're aiming for is realistic and achievable expectations for each type of relationship in your life.*

> *"Today, we turn to one person to provide what an entire village once did: a sense of grounding, meaning and continuity. At the same time, we expect our committed relationships to be romantic as well as emotionally and sexually fulfilling. Is it any wonder that so many relationships crumble under the weight of it all?"*
> ~Esther Perel, Psychotherapist

Stop thinking about your romantic partner as your boyfriend, girlfriend, lover, significant other, or whatever name you gave that role. Allow yourself to see them for who they are. Stop expecting them to fill a position you imagined for them, one for which they likely don't know the job description.

When we separate our relationships by giving them titles, much like job descriptions, we create a whole set of expectations for the person in that role. The trouble starts because we don't let the other person in on the requirements we've created. I mean, really, have you ever said: *"Sweetie, I love you with all my heart and I expect you to love me back even when I'm having a bad day and being really mean and whining on about this, that and the other. I expect you to be totally understanding of me even when you can see that I was the one at fault, that I was lazy, mean, or impatient. I expect you to be the person who soothes all my ruffled feathers, tells me I'm right and amazing and calms me down when I'm freaking out about something at work or something someone else did and I expect you to do this on my timetable, not yours and without ever letting your own problems, commitments or thoughts get in the way."*

I suspect not.

Yet, we do this all the time without realizing it.

All too often we've got one set of standards for friends, another for family and another more comprehensive and stricter set for our partners. Since we never *really* clue them into our expectations, they're bound to fail. This leads to us being upset or hurt and feeding the cycle of discontent and failed relationships.

The moment you give up expecting your partner to be *better than* or *more than* any other friend is the moment you shift into being in real partnership with that person. Seeing your romantic partner as a true friend, without any extended expectations of how they should behave or support you, will create space for the very kind of support you most want.

It may sound silly but think of romance like a potted plant. If you stick the plant in a small pot, forget to water it, and always shine the brightest light on it, that poor plant is never gonna bloom. But, move it to a bigger pot with rich soil, water it and feed it and give it enough light and shade to be happy, and you'll see the most amazing flowers showing up even in the dead of winter (this also works with semi-dead orchids).

We have to nurture our relationships and one way to do that is to look at the expectations we've placed upon each. Is what you're expecting from one type of relationship very different from all your others? If so... check that shit!

This isn't to say that each type of relationship shouldn't have different guidelines; for example, you don't expect your boss to be your friend, but maybe you're delighted that they're friendly. You don't expect your parents to agree with everything you do and maybe you see they support you in their own ways. You don't expect your friends to be there 110% of the time and more often than not they show up cheering you more frequently than you hoped.

Temper your expectations.

Take them out. Look at each one of them.

Ask yourself if you have the same expectation of your friends or your family?

Would you want that same expectation placed on you?

If so, hang onto it, if not... well go right ahead and toss that puppy out! It's not doing anyone any good. You'll surprise yourself when you let it go. You'll be creating a bigger, more generous pot with more space for growth and you'll see the flower of your romance, and all your relationships, bloom bigger and more colorfully than you imagined.

Tip

♦ *One of the most important relationships you have is the one with your Self. Take some time to look at how you're treating your Self and what your expectations are. Are they realistic and compassionate, or are there a whole lotta "should" and "need to" in there? Easing up can help you achieve the kinds of external relationships you truly desire.*

How to End Any Relationship

We've all had to exit a relationship at one time or another.

Whether it's a job, romance or friendship, at some point we have to come to grips with the fact that all relationships change with time. Sometimes the changes draw us deeper into engagement and other times we struggle because it's no longer a good fit. When the latter happens, the smartest and kindest action is to create a straightforward exit plan and bring the relationship to a close.

Let me be clear here—ending a relationship doesn't always mean you never engage with that person, team, or company again. It does mean that you make a clear break from the original terms of entanglement and craft a new agreement that serves you and allows you to move forward. It may mean no contact ever or could be the start of a different type of relationship with that person, people or job.

Sometimes it takes a review of the original contract or a discussion of agreements. Other times it can mean a complete break in communication for a period of time or for good. It all depends on the original agreements and expectations, and the outcome you desire, and what will support the new shape of the relationship best.

It doesn't always look like "all or nothing."

Here's an example:

Years ago, a friend came to me completely undone because she'd been told that her marriage was over. She'd been married for 25 years, loved her partner most of that time and while she'd been unhappy for a while, wasn't willing to end the marriage. What she saw ahead of her was an all-or-nothing choice; being partnered or being alone.

As she let loose with her fears I suggested that perhaps the "end" of her marriage was simply a letting go of the relationship as it had been and an opportunity to create a new relationship with her partner.

They were now at a point where they could choose to redefine what they wished to create together. She was willing to take a look at what she wanted moving forward and do the hard work (yes, it is work to shift the trajectory of a relationship) of letting go of what her marriage had looked like— what she expected it to continue to feel like into the distant future. Happily, so was her partner.

While it was challenging and painful at times, they each allowed themselves to release old ideas and expectations. Together they crafted a new relationship and deeper connection with each other. Today they are one of the happiest couples I know. Spend an afternoon with them and they exude appreciation and contentment which embraces everyone around them.

Ending relationships can involve some difficult conversations, and if you're willing to step into the lead, will allow you to aim your actions and responses toward your desired outcome.

A little planning goes a long way to creating a meeting, if not of the minds, at least a conversation where it's clear to all parties what's going to happen next. Being clear in what you're moving toward will help ease the breakup process whether you're breaking up with a boss, a job, a lover or a friend.

And again... breaking up only means an end to what was. You always have a choice in what you wish to create next.

Once you've decided to end a relationship, you'll probably experience a range of emotions as mapped out in the Five-Stage Kubler Ross Curve of Change: Shock, Anxiety, Overwhelm, Struggle (to find meaning), and finally... Moving on.

The best breakups happen when you have a clear set of action steps to take you through the process, so let's take a look at a simple 10-step process you can use to end any relationship.

10 Simple Steps to End a Relationship:

1. Meet the problem head-on. Stop denying there's a problem.

The first step is to see the relationship for what it is. Ditch all judgment and hopes about what you would like to have happen and take a clear-eyed view of what is going on that is not supporting you. This is the time to take off the rose-colored glasses and place your emotions to the side. You want to assess as clearly as possible the events that have led to the breakup.

Hint: If you find it hard to let go of the "If only..." then imagine your best friend describing the situation to you. What would you suggest they do?

2. Write it out!

Take five to fifteen minutes to list the emotions you're feeling. Don't get caught up in reasons, simply write them down so you see them clearly.

This is expressive writing and will help you get everything out on paper where you can see it. It'll also help you keep emotions out of the later discussion which will result in clearer communication on your part.

3. Support yourself.

Let a few key friends know what you're planning and make a date to meet up after the talk (if possible). Alternately, make a plan to go somewhere afterward that feels quiet and supportive to you—maybe a walk in a park or near a river. Perhaps meeting a friend for a beverage or a movie. Whatever you choose, make a firm plan to check in with a friend who will hold you to your plan.

4. Arrange a time to talk.

Set up a time that works for you and the other person. State simply that you want to sit down with them for a conversation. Say that it will take about 45 minutes and you want to be able to give each person space to talk. Do not get sucked into a discussion beforehand. You want to give both of you time to settle and you're not trying to catch the other person off-guard. Make sure the time and location are quiet and you both feel safe and can speak freely.

Hint: You want to approach the set-up with as much kindness and respect as you would want for yourself.

5. Meet in person.

Explain that you've given it a lot of thought and recognize that the relationship has ended. Avoid blaming anyone. Express your thoughts and accept your part in how the relationship has shifted. Be kind and very clear that it is over.

6. Allow responses.

Remember, you're the one bringing this out into the open. Allow the other person some time to respond. There may be surprise, tears, anger, or other emotions from the other person. Listen and hold firm to your decision. If possible, allow yourself to feel gratitude and respect for the other person; this may be difficult for both parties and when we view the other person through empathic eyes, it's easier to hold our own decisions with compassion.

7. Allow questions.

Allow the other person to ask whatever questions they need to. Answer whatever you can calmly and compassionately. Do not defend or explain your actions. You can respond to 99% of questions by stating why the relationship no longer is a good fit *for you* without laying blame on anyone. Hold firm to the 45-minute timeframe for the conversation and don't fall into arguing or justifying your position. It won't help and can complicate the discussion.

8. Follow through.

Give the other person time to digest the information, and if necessary, schedule a follow-up conversation to discuss practicalities at a specific time. Know that there may need to be follow-up conversations to organize the logistics of projects.

9. Final words.

Be clear that the relationship is ending and that you will not be in contact for a period of at least 30 days (frankly, I recommend three months of zero contact unless you need to connect for logistics around work, projects, pets, or kids). You want to give both parties time to fully absorb the changes and find their way forward.

Do not poke, ping, prod, or "like" someone's posts on social media. Do not text or otherwise connect with them for at least 30 days. If you find this difficult then remove them from your phone, unfriend them and/or unfollow them. You're not being "kind" by continuing to connect after you have broken up. The same goes for a work relationship. You might really love the project or the team you just left, but let them have time to get over your departure before you try to reconnect on new terms.

10. Don't chase the tiger's tail.

Once you have ended a relationship, take time to reflect on it in writing. Allow yourself to celebrate any sweetness or positive aspects as well as lament any negative ones. Write out (in longhand if possible), what you see now that you didn't see or didn't want to see earlier in the relationship. By reflecting upon the whole, you allow yourself to appreciate what worked and what didn't, so you don't repeat the pattern.

As you move into future relationships, whether work or personal, don't chase the tiger's tail. By this I mean don't aim to solve what went wrong with the last relationship in the new one.

It's super easy to fall into this trap and we've all done it! We have a boss who yells so we take a job with a boss who is soft spoken. We ended a romance with someone who went along with everything we said, only to start up with someone who challenges us. In each case, we were trying to solve the problem from the past inside of the present. Not only is this impossible, but it sets us up for continual failure since we're never paying attention to what is actually happening in the present.

In your next relationship, whatever that may be, pay attention to what you feel and who you are being in it. If something's not working, have a talk about it as soon as you see it. If you don't like who you are being in the relationship, now you have all the steps to leave thoughtfully laid out for you.

SECTION FOUR

The Tough Questions

The tough questions are the ones without answers or the ones which offer a pyramid of possible answers far too complex for easy agreement. Sometimes we don't even agree on the questions. These are the existential questions. The ones that have kept philosophers, the religious, and seekers of all kinds busy since the beginning, whenever the beginning was.

"Who am I?"

"What is my purpose?"

And often a tad belatedly... "Why did I do that?"

Whether we dive into philosophy or belief, the existential questions can be the most interesting, nail-biting, frustrating, and satisfying ones to explore. At first, these may seem to be questions that are irrelevant to daily life. After all, we still need to work, pay bills, cook food, etc... what good would it do to ask the seemingly unanswerable?

Allowing ourselves to play in the sea of deep questions helps us identify and live into clarity. We can discover who we are and what we're about. Asking these questions helps us become better at discerning what's truly important to our well-being and what might be mere ripples on the surface.

"You're the sky. Everything else – it's just the weather."
~ *Pema Chödrön, Buddhist teacher, author, and nun.*

Taking time to understand who our Self really is, makes it a helluva lot easier to aim towards enriching life and away from being drained emotionally, mentally and physically. Exploring the vastness of possibility expands us while allowing us to set markers along the journey as a kind of mental breadcrumb trail to mark our way forward.

I'm not talking about religiousness here. Though my own story does start with a reference to religion, what I'm on about is exploring the landscape of how we get to know ourselves from the inside out, instead of believing the reflection that others give back to us. It's too easy to forget that we're the territory *and* the map, other people reflect imperfect versions of us back to ourselves. They show the "us" that they see through their own set of filters; colored by how they would like us to be, or how they feel about what we do or say, or what we think or believe.

A little background will probably be helpful here...

My brother and I were raised as free-thinkers. Our parents presented us with a smattering of religions and cultural ideas from around the world, a brief and rather general overview of key points, and then told us to do as we saw fit. This meant that I spent one summer reading the Bible, a few family holidays trying to figure out why roughly half my relatives went to synagogue or Hebrew classes and the other half held a Ukrainian family picnic every July and consumed mass quantities of homemade kielbasa and birch beer in between powerboat trips 'round the lake. I dedicated tons of weekends to plowing my way through travel and art books as well as reading my way right-to-left through my father's shelves of philosophy and psychology texts.

I burrowed into new ideas about who and how we are and why we do things the way we do. What drives us and what causes or changes our reaction to the world? These were the questions that often kept me awake, bleary-eyed, and finger-cramped from writing. I wanted to know all the *whys* and that meant I was exploring all the *whats*—trying things out—testing the existential waters by tossing ideas into the ocean of people around me to see which ones floated and which sank.

Music played a big part in my explorations. As a kid I played a variety of instruments from cello and piano to flute, none with any particular interest, all well enough to occasionally play with others. My real passion is singing. I adore harmonizing with people and have often been so carried away harmonizing that I've joined voices with opera singers on midnight summer evenings in Italian piazzas, with Swiss goatherders near Luzerne before sharing bread, cheese and honey, and with bluegrass bands in several states. I've sung old-timey harmonies with a circle of people I passed while walking my dog one afternoon and with some well-known musicians in open jam sessions around the country. Music and harmony are ways I can experience someone else's traditions and get a taste of their world. The way we sing, the way we create or play music, tells a lot about what we value as beautiful, important, or inventive. Through music (and all forms of creative expression...), we come to know ourselves and tell the world about our experiences in life.

I sang in a variety of glee clubs and choirs throughout childhood and into my high school years (at which point I switched from organized choirs to disorganized jam sessions).

The choirs often traveled to churches for festivals like Christmas and Easter. We heard the masses, provided the music, and often spent the hours before performances singing in the streets (much to our choir directors' dismay).

Synagogues, churches, meditation centers, yoga practices and kirtans, circles of musicians in parks and piazzas, and all the conversations that arose in these congregations of people increased my curiosity. I wanted to understand what different people believed and why. How did their thinking impact their lives? What difference did their faith or belief make on a daily basis and what the heck was the difference between "having faith" and "believing in" something?

Those last two ideas, "having faith" and "believing in" something, create a series of deeply engaging roads of thought to wind our way down when we apply them to the questions of *Who am I? What is my purpose? Why did I do that?* Allowing yourself to play along these paths, without assuming there is an answer to be had, invites you to see and understand far more than if you begin the journey with a destination in mind.

I offer the following as one way to think about belief and faith.

When we "believe in" an idea or a person we tie ourselves to whatever is on offer. We toss our proverbial coins in their cup and allow them to set the agenda and limitations for us. In effect, we give up some autonomy in trade for a thought that someone suggested was worth following. We follow as long as it continues to feed us and we think we have a destination in mind—or at the very least, a benefit we'll receive for believing. The trouble arises when we don't receive whatever benefits we think we were promised.

On the other hand, when we have faith in an idea or person, we retain our freedom. Having faith implies a measure of willingness to *hope* that something or other will manifest and yet allows the possibility that it may not come to pass. Having faith requires us to decide our actions, to choose our own path at some level, and to be continually seeking, rather than aiming for, a specific benefit or destination. We are less apt to be let down, or perhaps less frustrated and annoyed if our faith is not met with fruition. For example, I can have faith that people will act politely but I'm not terribly surprised when they don't. However, if I believe that people will act politely, when they're rude I'm apt to feel a deeper annoyance than if I'd had faith in them.

I invite you into faith when you ask the question *Who am I?* Start out disbelieving that you know the answer and instead imagine that you have arrived from far, far away. You've landed here and the first being you meet is YOU. Imagine what meeting YOU for the very first time would be like. You might listen to the sounds of breathing coming from YOU. If your hearing was keen you'd also hear a rhythmic pattern from the center of YOU (heartbeat). You'd notice movements, a fluttering (eyelashes), expansion and contraction (arms stretching outward); everything you notice you do not yet have a name for and observe nonetheless. After some time you find a way to communicate with YOU and you learn more than the mere physical form. Spend enough time in communication and you have a deeper sense of knowing, one that might include the feel of YOU against your own body, the ways that this YOU thinks about internal and external worlds, and most importantly how this YOU defines who they are. Allow yourself to observe all these aspects of this YOU without judgment. What are the areas where you and this YOU diverge? Where do you agree?

When you've really allowed yourself to know YOU, you've created an opportunity to choose how you want to be in the world from this moment forward. It's when you see yourself for who you truly are, as objectively as possible, that you become aware of more choices that exist. Knowing these, how then do you choose to be in the world? Which actions create experiences of comfort, magic, happiness, or joy, and which ones move you further away?

As you consciously create experiences you desire, you embody your purpose. Purpose is a funny word in this context because it implies a need to be doing, i.e., doing *something* rather than *being* something. *I'm gonna toss ya a radical idea...* what if your purpose is simply to BE? What could that mean? Humans are "beings" not "doings," hence the name "human beings." *It's funny when you think of it, we don't say, tiger-beings or ant-beings or oak tree-beings, yet every living thing is BE-ing.* Something in us must have wanted reminding that we are BE-ing all the time. We don't usually see this as a conscious choice, we ARE, or we ARE NOT—but if you're reading this, you most definitely ARE.

The third question, *Why did I do that?* is easier to answer when you understand who you are and how you're being in the world. It's a tricky sort of answer though because it answers two different and related understandings of "why."

The first response might come from knowing what you think is pleasurable and what you deem as uncomfortable or icky. In general, when you aren't paying too much attention, you move toward whatever you've decided is enjoyable or gratifying and attempt to avoid the unpleasant like suffering, pain, disgust, etc... Most often you make these shifts toward or away as though they were dance moves, fluidly sliding from one direction to another without much conscious attention. For example, if you like chocolate and dislike coffee, you'll order hot cocoa over a cuppa joe every time. If you prefer watching a movie to taking a hike, you'll spend more time indoors than out. You get the idea. It takes conscious effort to move in the direction of something you've decided you do not desire or like.

The second level of *Why did I do that?* is simpler and more radical. If you imagine that your Self is here on the planet to explore, then by your very nature your Self wants to have tons of different adventures. Think of your Self as an infinite, eternal, and whole energy which greedily desires every possible experience. The transformation of growing up from a small body into a bigger body is one series of expansions. The variety of work you do is another set of experiences. Any accidents, heartbreaks, sadness, anger, joy, elation, or delight; all of these are experiences. So the deeper answer to *Why did I do that?* is because your Self wanted to feel something you had never felt before, or you craved the familiar, no matter how painful or crappy it was the first time.

Whatever you did in the past has gotten you what you have in the present. To create a different future you've got to do something you've never done before. The bigger risk is staying on the side of life's river you already know, rather than crossing into unknown territory. Choosing radically different actions feel prickly and uncomfortable until they become your new habit, your new way of BE-ing. When you reach that point you're living your new normal.

The idea that you aim toward what you already know is an old truism in psychology and in human adaptation. When you have survived an event or a big change, your body/brain then has proof that no matter how painful or crappy the experience was, you're likely to survive it again. Whether it's heartache, playing small in life, staying in partnerships that don't feel wonderful, or jobs that leave you feeling "less than," if you *know* it, it can feel like the "better" choice because moving into unknown territory feels itchy, uncomfortable and scary—until it doesn't.

Bundle the three questions together and let yourself feel into the answers for a surefire way to break old habits that keep you stuck, limited by a job or relationship that doesn't serve you, or fill your heart with a passionate, fiery drive. Most of the time, we forget that we *always* have a choice. Sometimes we don't like the options AND... the choice still exists. When you're faced with a choice and aren't crazy about either side, take a moment to imagine that you don't have a choice at all—does not having a choice feel better or worse than the choice in front of you?

When you know who you are and you see what you're choosing to believe, you'll see plenty of options for action. Recognizing that you have choices on everything from how to dress, how to spend your time or money, and even how to feel, you demonstrate faith in yourself. Having faith means that you can always grow, change and create the kinds of experiences and the kind of life you most desire.

Finding Meaning

Make a list of the ten things that make you deep-down, dancing-round-the-living-room-or-kitchen happy.

Write them down.

Read through them twice. Change whatever feels like you wrote it to impress someone else like your partner or parent, your uncle Ralph or that friend who always seems to have everything figured out.

Add to your list anything that matters to you (and only you). It's okay if what you write feels big or little... Small and large, it's important to YOU!

Maybe it's adventure traveling or trying every restaurant or take-out place in town. You might include times when you connect with friends, family, or community. You can add things like reading a book, building or fixing something, taking time to walk in the woods, or simply being goofy and playing dominos or jacks. No matter what you write, each one is an opportunity to create happiness and growth for yourself.

Read over your list of ten items and commit to doing five percent more of each one this year.

Each year, review and revise your list. Keep it relevant to the person you are NOW.

Include only items that make you feel truly joyful, connected, delighted, and which hold deep meaning for *you*.

Tips

♦ *Let your list guide you to create a life you love now and one you'll still want to be living in five or ten years. Don't make it a list of accomplishments (that's a different list).*

♦ *If you find yourself smiling when you add an item, you're "doing it right."*

Write Your Personal Manifesto

You can't know what you want to achieve if you don't clarify who you are and what's truly, madly, deeply important to you. By creating a personal manifesto or mission statement for yourself, based on your core values, you'll be able to define your goals more clearly and more aligned with who you truly are, deep down in your heart, which... by the way, is where it really counts.

Write Your Personal Manifesto

Start with 15 minutes of writing. You can always write more as your ideas take hold.

Breathe deeply a couple times, then take yourself on a

mental walk backward through your last 5 years. Jot down challenges you've met, goals you've reached, failures that have taught you valuable lessons. Notice who you were being in those moments. What were you doing, what actions did you take or choose not to take?

What types of challenges are you drawn to in general? What do you gravitate towards? What are the core values that make you who you are? What themes or situations repeatedly show up for you? What makes you giggle and what makes you feel all warm and fuzzy inside?

After a few minutes, reflect on when you feel powerful, vulnerable, at ease, and most yourself. Remember, you're not simply driven by money or success; what else has made you who you are today? What empowers you, what motivates you?

What do you know is true and what do you believe in?

You can start with:

I believe... and *I know in my bones this is true...*

Once you've got a rough version drafted, read over what you've written and highlight the statements that you feel most passionate and connected to. You know—the ones that feel like they come straight from your heart.

Stuck?

Here's an example from mine:

> *I stand for truth, honesty, and courage. I stand for waking the fuck up. I stand for seeing the choices in front of us and consciously making a choice that moves us towards a desired future. I stand for making choices, even when they're hard; even when all the options might seem to suck.*
>
> *I stand for being human. I stand for communication*

and connecting people to each other for the benefit of all. I believe in telling the truth even when people don't want to hear it. I am all for rocking the boat because the status quo isn't good enough.

I believe in community. I believe in compassion. I believe in open-mindedness. I believe that we can all figure out how to get along, even when we have differences in opinion, beliefs, or culture.

I create a world filled with joy, delight, and deep connections. I encourage people to run barefooted down muddy paths, wade in ponds, swim rivers, and dive into cold oceans in the middle of winter. I inspire people to be brave for themselves. I spark people's hearts to race with excitement at what they do every single day.

Now that you've got the idea, go find a quiet place where you won't be disturbed. Grab coffee, tea, cookies, or a sandwich and give yourself permission to dive in deep, write from your heart, and be wildly inspired in your statements. Embrace who you truly are and state clearly how you intend to show up in the world.

Tips

♦ *Core values are the ways we are BE-ing in the world that are non-negotiable. They're the core of your heart, the ways you show up in the world without thinking. They're the drivers of your actions and the aspects of you that shape your thoughts. You have many core values, but for now hone in on your top three. Get to know them so well you can recite them in under 10 seconds when asked.*

♦ *Still stuck? Check out the worksheet in the Resources Section.*

Change Your Self

Well... not really....

This is really about creating the life you want by changing the way you "do" you.

There's an understanding in Positive Psychology that says we can change "how I do me" by starting at one of the following three places.

We can:

1. Change our thinking to change behavior or emotional response.
2. Change our behavior to alter emotional response and thinking.
3. Change our emotional response to alter thinking and behavior.

By shifting any one of these "break-points" in the system, we create change for ourselves. It's up to us to decide in what direction we want the change to flow. We aim towards a positive or negative direction depending on what we choose to pay attention to.

Change Your Thinking

The first way you can hack your Self is by changing your thinking. Research from the field of Positive Psychology has proven that we humans create more of whatever we focus on. This means that if you're spending all your time examining why you hate your job, why your team sucks, or what is wrong in any of your relationships, you'll create more of those negative experiences *because* you're paying attention to them. When you shift your focus to what *is* working, what *is* going well, and what *does* feel great then you create more positive experiences.

Focusing on the positive has a beneficial effect on your physical and mental health. Data supports practices like daily gratitude journaling, filling a "Joy Jar" with your accomplishments, and otherwise acknowledging positive aspects of your life, all having positive effects.

When we choose to focus on what *is* working, we see new options and new solutions that create more desirable outcomes. By identifying what is helping a situation we continue the trend toward success by taking more of those actions and literally seeing more opportunities.

Celebrating and acknowledging when things go well builds confidence and keeps us moving forward towards our goals, while berating ourselves or complaining about what is not working moves us further away. The more we focus on what is effective and positive the more we create a growth mindset that shifts us out of beliefs and behaviors that undermine our success.

Focusing on what is working is not the same as "positive thinking." What we're talking about is taking action. Every step that moves you forward is a physical activity, whether it's writing a note, making a call, meeting with someone, etc... the key to creating more of what *is* working is to continually take physical action that creates change. Thinking about things doesn't create change, nor does "deciding" or "trying" to do something. The only thing that achieves goals is by taking physical steps toward fulfillment of those goals.

I hear some of you arguing about the need for planning and preparation. Yes! We also need to plan and prepare. Both plans and preparations require physical actions, you've got to write lists of what needs to happen, and who is responsible for which parts. You'll often have to contact people to make things happen. No goal was ever reached simply by thinking about it!

If your goal is to change something about how you do your life, start by writing out what you want to be doing. Don't waste time writing about what is not working or what you don't like. Write what you *do* want.

Whether you jot bullet points, write in prose, poetry, diagrams, sketches, or record voice memos and transcribe them, you're getting the thoughts out of your head, in front of your eyes and that'll allow you to see what action step you need to take next.

Beliefs are simply thoughts you have thunk so often
you think they're true.

The hardest aspect of changing how you do life is seeing where your thoughts have become rules you're now following (we can also call these *beliefs*). Until you look at the beliefs that drive your behavior, you can't change a thing. This is where some hard work and a coach can come in handy. Roll up your sleeves, be willing to get muddy, and start pulling out anything that looks like an idea that you feel you *have to* adhere to. You're searching for statements and ideas about the type of person you think you are or have to be. These can include statements like, "I'm shy." "I'm not good at writing, or maths." "I'd never be able to do... or to be...." Go slowly, be aware that these statements are like snakes in tall grass—they're slippery to catch and they'll twist and turn in your hands, looking like truisms rather than the mere thoughts that they are.

The rules we make for ourselves are the beliefs (ideas) we have embedded into our hearts about who we are. We can change our beliefs by removing these thorny ideas and healing our hearts.

Hunt for your own ideas about your Self. "I've had a wonderful/terrible life so far." "I would never/always do..." "I'm the kind of person who..." These are the kinds of beliefs or rules you're working to uncover. These are what drive your behavior. In order to change your life, you'll need to examine your beliefs, rules, and thoughts. Are they helping or hindering you?

Easy Steps to Uncover Hidden Beliefs:

1. Set a timer for four minutes.

2. Writing as fast as you can, finishing the following sentence fragment: "I am..."

3. At the end of four minutes. Go back through your list and mark all the words or statements that help you be your best Self with a ▷ and all the ones that hinder you with a □.

Any that you mark with a ▷ are helping you towards your best self. You want to take a good look at these and find ways to apply them more often in your life. The ones you marked with a □ you can choose whether to let go of. By releasing ideas that hinder you, you heal the places in your heart that have been wounded. In choosing to let go of whatever doesn't serve you any longer, you create space for yourself to expand into the person who does the types of things that people like you really want to achieve in life. Whether you want to create a wildly successful business, be more patient, be more excited about your job, etc... What you're seeking is supported by growth and expansion, not by staying small and limited, stuck in old ideas or stale beliefs.

Head's Up!

Change is uncomfortable! It has to be or it would not be Change with a capital "C." If you do what you always did you'll get what you have right now. As you shift your thinking and behavior, you're likely to feel as though you're pushing a block up a mountain. Don't panic! The mountain and the block will get smaller. Be willing to stick it out in the uncomfortable spaces, soon enough they'll be the new normal and you'll wonder why you spent time doing it "the old way."

Change Your Behavior

The second way to hack how you do you is to hack your behavior. Changing behavior is often the quickest way to see positive shifts and reach your desired outcome. To do this you're going to lean heavily on your imagination because your imagination not only creates, it stores everything you've experienced the same way a painter stockpiles different tubes of paint. Imagination is what you tap when you open the drawer and pull out some new colors to paint with.

Start by imagining your desired outcome or goal (and nope... this is not about the power of positive thinking!). Maybe you want to be less anxious, or more patient. Maybe you want to be more successful or less shy. Perhaps you want to create a new business or find a more exciting job. No matter what you desire, the first step is to clarify it for yourself. Write the change you desire in one clear sentence.

Now that's done, bring to mind someone who embodies that quality, or the qualities of someone who runs that business, or has that career. We'll call this person your Guide. It can be someone you know personally or a public or fictional figure. Imagine you're standing in front of your guide, observing them. Notice how they stand, how they talk, how they walk. Practice emulating all the physical characteristics you notice. How does your Guide smile, or laugh? What gestures do they make? How do they dress? Let yourself get really granular in your observations. Make some notes and move on to asking them a few key questions.

Warning! This can feel weird the first couple of times you do it. That's okay! You're breaking boundaries here and tossing old habits and thoughts out the window! Remember, it's going to feel weird if you're doing something new. Keep doing anything and pretty soon it'll stop feeling weird and just be how you do things.

Imagine standing in front of your Guide and ask them some questions out loud (yes, I said out loud!). You can ask for advice or ideas about how they do what they do. For example, if you're wanting to shift from being shy to being outgoing you might ask, "What do you know about yourself that helps you feel confident?" or "What do you do first thing in the morning?" You could ask what advice they have for you or ask, "What can you tell me about being confident and outgoing?" Trust whatever answers your imagination tosses back to you. The answers might come as words or as images. They might arise in you as emotions. However they show up, make some notes and then use the information to create some action steps.

Your imagination is part of your sensory system and creates a mental catalog of everything you've experienced. When you tap your imagination for answers, it retrieves all the information related to your query and pulls it together in a form you can access. What you get when you ask a question is all the information you have ever observed. To paraphrase marketing guru Seth Godin, "People like us do things like this." We can use our very human habit of cataloging everything around us to teach ourselves new ways of being and doing. Because we can imagine acting "as if," we can teach ourselves how to be different in the world.

Now that you have some advice from your Guide, create a list of actions that'll help move you into *doing you* in a new way. Turn your list into physical actions you commit to. Take it slowly and work on one action at a time. The key to success is repetition, repetition, repetition. Repeat the action until it feels totally natural and you no longer have to think about doing it, then move on to the next one.

As you complete each action, check it off and find a way to celebrate your ongoing transformation. You might add them as "wins" to your Joy Jar or daily gratitude record. This type of behavioral shift can feel slow at times. Acknowledging each step of change *as you go* will keep you motivated.

Quick Actions to Boost Positivity:

1. Keep a daily gratitude record.

Each day record at least one thing you're grateful for. Who was involved, what occurred, what did you do, what emotions did you feel, and how did your body feel?

2. Start a Joy Jar.

You'll need a large jar or bowl and some slips of paper.

Each day write at least one thing that made you laugh, smile, or was an accomplishment. They can be big or small, simple or complex. Place each note in the jar. At the end of the week pull out a few notes and let yourself drink in all the positivity. You can put them back in the jar and continually feed your jar-o-joy.

3. Make a Happiness Playlist.

Create a playlist of songs that make ya wanna shout with joy. Every day choose a song, take a break, dance around, sing at the top of your lungs and let yourself delight in the happy goodness.

4. Be Neighborly.

Research shows that when we do nice things for others, we feel happier and healthier. Being neighborly, doing something nice for someone, no matter how small the act, boosts our immune system and fills our internal "happiness bucket." Aim to do one nice thing for someone as often as possible.

5. Get outside.

Whether you take a five-minute sunbath standing outside your job, or a longer stroll down the street, in a park, or on a trail somewhere—being outside in sunlight will boost your happiness and physical health by a measurable amount. Walking or moving will double the effect so go ahead and throw in a little outdoor dance for yourself in between projects or tasks.

Change Your Emotions

This really should be called, "Change Your Responses" because what we're really changing is the response we have when emotions arise. From a purely biological standpoint, emotions are chemistry. A particular mix of chemicals will create a physiologic experience that we name as a particular emotion. The action we take next is the *response* to the chemical soup coursing through our bodies.

While we don't have much conscious control over the chemical mix, we have 100% control over our own response. We can cry or yell, laugh, giggle, smack something or go curl up in bed. We can choose any number of possible responses to an emotion and then choose the next actions we take.

> *"It is our compulsive reaction to the situations in which we are placed that causes stress."*
> ~Sadhguru Jaggi Vasudev, Inner Engineering:
> A Yogi's Guide to Joy

We are always responding, all the time, to everything that is happening around us, whether we think it directly affects us or not. We can't help but respond. For example, we can't choose to breathe the air or have our hearts beat in response to living. We *can* choose our reactions and the actions we take. Each of those choices directly affects how we think and behave.

When we notice and name our emotions, we increase our awareness of our reactions. Now we have more control over what happens next. We have more choices. We *can* choose to heat things up or calm things down based on the action we take next. By creating a pause between response and action, we effectively increase our ability to think more clearly about the outcome we desire and how to move towards and not away from it.

Four Steps to Happier Outcomes

1. When an emotion arises, notice it and exhale three times. Remember that old tune... "Three, that's the magic number..."

Don't do anything except breathe. You're giving yourself time to notice which emotion or emotions arise, what reaction you had, and you're creating space before you take any action.

2. When you feel your body calming, ask yourself what outcome you desire in the situation.

3. Next ask yourself, "What physical action will move me closer to that desired outcome?"

4. Take that action. Repeat steps three and four until the outcome is reached.

Check the resources for additional practices to support all these techniques.

Tips

♦ See **Best Self Exercise** in Resources section at the end of this book.

♦ Not sure which emotions are coming up for you? Check the **List of Emotions** in the Resources section.

♦ See **Acting "As If" Exercise** in the Resources section at the end of this book.

♦ Fun Fact: If you want to learn to paint like a specific painter, use the same technique of emulating the gestures, how the artist put the paint on the canvas, the brushstrokes and eventually you'll understand how and why the *painting looks the way it does, and how to replicate it. This is one of the ways that acting "as if" proves useful.*

https://meteoreducation.com/how-does-thinking-positive-thoughts-affect-neuroplasticity/ and https://hbr.org/2015/09/the-powerful-effect-of-noticing-good-things-at-work

The Origami of Life

Most of the time we don't think of folding paper as a USEFUL thing to spend time on. And... stop for a moment and think about it from a new perspective.

Origami requires you to be fully present in the moment.

When folding paper into intricate forms you've got to be fully aware and 100% responsible for what you're doing. Let your mind drift for a moment and your design falls apart or fails to spread its wings when completed.

From paper flowers and animals to abstract forms, the requirements of origami are exactly those that build resilience in us as we practice them.

Being Resilient Allows Us To:
♦ *Be flexible;*
♦ *Recover quickly from adversity;*

172

- *Practice responsibility;*
- *Be fully present to whatever shows up;*
- *Access inner strengths; and*
- *Respond with considered action.*

How do these relate to origami?

Flexibility:

When you begin with the idea of making a new thing out of an old thing, you have no choice but to be flexible. You imagine that a simple sheet of paper could become something three-dimensional and then make it so.

Adversity:

As you fold the paper, whether you're following instructions or your own playfulness, you may find at some point that a fold or crease isn't quite right. You unfold it, flatten the paper down, and re-fold it so that the paper forms your imagined shape. This moves you through adversity.

Presence:

The form in your hands grows and with it, your awareness of being fully present. With paper-folding, if you look away or stop paying attention, the shape goes awry.

Strength:

The more you remain present, the more you bring your strengths into play. The precision, attention, patience, playfulness, and attitude you bring to the process are, by definition, your strengths. The more attention you pay to which strengths show up, the more you elevate them.

Responsibility and Action:

You are 100% responsible for whatever form your origami and your life take. Being response-able means you are always responding to whatever is happening around you, and that you are able to choose what action, (or non-action), to take next. Responsibility is not about blame.

You'll increase your resilience each time you practice these steps. The more you practice, the more resilient you become. The more resilient you are, the more you'll find yourself not being tossed upon the ocean of life's vicissitudes. You'll feel calmer, and more able to sail through whatever happens, and you'll see which actions will consistently move you towards your goals.

Find Your
Personal Payoff

Many times, we hear, "Begin with your why." No matter what aspect of business or life we're working to grow, common thinking is to define our goals and understand *why* we are creating whatever we are creating, or *why* someone wants to buy or participate in what we have to offer.

WHY is the easiest place to get bogged down and grumble to a grinding halt.

Rather than starting with "why," begin by naming your personal payoff. Whatever you want to create, offer or do has some sort of payoff for you personally (otherwise, you'd never aim to do it). When you get clear on the benefits (AKA: payoff) *to you*, you'll have uncovered a powerful motivator. That is a WHAT, not a WHY.

Now that you are clear on what will feel like measurable success for you personally, as opposed to what you can do for clients or the world, take it a step further and get clear on what goal you are aiming for, for yourself.

When you clarify *what* your goal is, you'll more easily identify the action steps you need to create that outcome. The necessary answers can arrive as you move forward (not in advance of starting).

Finding your personal payoff encourages clarity and action. Knowing **what** your payoff is makes it easier to see the action steps you need to take to achieve your goals.

As you move into action, you'll notice something... Almost by magic, the reasons *why* start showing up, and (here's the best part) they'll feel more authentic and motivating than if you'd started with *why* in the first place.

When you know **what** you're working for—**what** you're wanting to create in your business, relationship or life—it's easier to stay motivated when things go haywire (or take four times as long as you hoped). Is your payoff an amount of money? Is it the freedom to travel, or time with your family? Something you haven't clarified? Go ahead and name it right now. You can always change it later if it doesn't feel aligned.

Whether your payoff is something concrete or an experience, whether it's freedom or the ability to create something completely new for yourself, knowing exactly **what** you want to create will lead you more directly to what your heart most desires.

The next time you find yourself stuck, whatever it is... don't ask *why?*

Ask WHAT!

Self-Care

Self-care is a term that's gotten so overloaded with different descriptions, that it can feel impossible to know what you're supposed to do for yourself. What would really be self-care? Is it spa days, hikes, a vacation in Cabo, or someone else to do your chores?

Ask one person and you'll hear that self-care is about eating better, getting more rest, and making sure you exercise regularly. Somebody else says it's about meditating, taking soothing baths, and giving yourself some slack. The next person tells you to redesign your schedule, spend more time with friends or read more uplifting books. All of these can be considered "self-care" and they each skip over a deeper well of appreciation we can draw from.

The underlying element of self-care is self-compassion. Whether you choose to be nicer to yourself in speech, action, or thought, what you're doing is being more compassionate with yourself. Taking time off, slowing down, paying attention to how you feel or how you talk to yourself—all these are ways to express compassion, appreciation, and love for yourself, and are honestly some of the most useful and valuable things you can do for yourself.

Allow yourself to have fun, laugh, and appreciate all the wonderful, silly, messy, dumb, difficult, or strange things you do. Acknowledge how much you learn about the world and other people and you'll build a foundation based on what you've learned. The more you acknowledge what you create each minute of every day, the more you aim yourself toward feeling successful, enriched, and wonderfully aligned and authentic.

The more you pay attention to what is working, the more success you'll create.

Creating (or carving out) space to relax, regroup, and re-ground demonstrates appreciation for yourself. You're also meeting your own needs, first by taking time to identify them, then by moving into action that fulfills them. Adding fun into the mix keeps your heart light and will help you move forward on days when you feel less than excited about taking time for yourself.

Looking for some ideas for heart-nourishing self-care? You're invited to check out the list below and dive in. Brainstorm—add ideas that suit you, mix-n-match, and create your own as you go. Remember: the best way to create what you want is to do it one step at a time!

Self-Care Suggestions:

♦ Take two minutes in the morning to acknowledge, out loud (yes! out loud!), something that went well in the past seven days. Linger on how it feels as you say it. Here's a starter for you: "I feel great because..."

♦ Set yourself up for less stress by kicking your para-sympathetic nervous system into gear with this super-quick breathwork practice. Exhale fully, inhale easily and smoothly, filling your lungs but not straining, exhale completely. Repeat three times. Do this practice a couple times a day and you'll feel the benefits of lowered stress.

♦ At the end of the day, write down three things that went well that day and what action you took that allowed each one. For example, I had an awesome walk with my dog because I set aside time in my schedule to do so. Or: It was a wonderfully sunny day because I allowed myself five minutes at lunch to stand up, stretch and notice the sky. At the end of the week, review and appreciate how much actually went your way and what you did to allow, acknowledge or create the successes.

♦ Set aside at least 1 day a month to do something fun. Aim for something that doesn't require a lot of money or a lot of planning: a picnic in the park, a walk 'round the local lake or museum will do. The key is to make it something easy and enjoyable for yourself.

♦ Buy some good quality moisturizer or body oil and once a week really go to town and pamper yourself. Take a relaxing shower or bath then let your body drink up the love as you smooth on your potion of choice. If you feel awkward doing this, imagine that you're smoothing the oil onto someone you love, someone you feel deserves to be appreciated and cared for. As time goes on, you'll find that you're more able to accept this for yourself.

- Add one new physical activity to your day. Take a walk, bike ride or snowshoe, dance to your fave jams, or head to the gym—anything that gets you moving in a new way. If you already do these things, find a new location or new activity that inspires you. By keeping things fresh you'll wake your brain up to what's interesting and possible.

- Spend at least 5 minutes in meditation each day. If you already have a meditation practice, you may want to freshen it up or rededicate yourself by appreciating the benefits you already enjoy. New to meditation? See the resource section in this book for some free guided meditations. (And remember—it's always a practice session, never a "Done" meditation session!)

- Set aside time each month to explore something or someplace new. Explore somewhere new and close by or someplace you've visited often and allow yourself to pay closer attention.

- Have a pot-luck with friends. Engaging and building community can be one of the most soul-nourishing things you do.

- Make a list of 12 new things you'd like to try this year and do one each month. Jot a few quick notes for each:
  - I did this...
  - I experienced...
  - I felt...
  - I want...

At the end of each month (and at the end of the year) spend a bit of time reviewing your experiences. What did you gain, which would you do again, which ones were the most interesting and fun?

- Watch a two-minute comedy sketch or funny video.
- Don't eat at your desk or workspace (not even if you work from home!). Go to another room or outdoors and change your view. You'll raise your energy level and shift perspective at the same time. I promise you'll return to work feeling refreshed and energized.
- Say something kind to yourself every day, at least once a day.
- Say something kind to someone else every day. Texting counts!!
- Give yourself permission to be truly and totally silly for five minutes every day.

Tips

- *Check out the resources section at the end of this book for free guided meditations.*
- *Research in Positive Psychology shows that when we demonstrate appreciation and kindness to others, we also reap a measurable benefit in positive and uplifting feelings.*
- *The Para-sympathetic Nervous System, (PNS) is known as the "rest and digest" system in our bodies. Triggering it into action, the PNS lowers stress hormones, relaxes muscles, and gives our physical bodies a kind of quickie spa treatment. By shifting from "fight, flight or freeze" into*

"rest, relax and recuperate" we experience less wear and tear on the body and a rejuvenated feeling of more energy and clarity.

How to Be Resilient

Resilience is our ability to bounce back and grow ourselves through the challenges.

There's a lot of talk about resilience these days. It's definitely become a "thing" and that translates to many people feeling as though they have to take a class, do a webinar or get some kind of certification from someone else in order to be resilient.

That's fine if you want to further your education or take on the larger scope of community resilience, but if you want to be more personally resilient, keep reading. I'm offering you a list of practical ways to increase your resilience. All are simple. Some can feel easy or challenging depending on the day, your mood, or the weather and stress level you're experiencing.

Read, contemplate or practice—whatever serves you. The

bottom line is that the more you consider, play within and actually practice the techniques, the more confident, resilient, and courageous you'll find yourself BE-ing in the world.

10 Ways to Increase Your Resilience

1. Laugh at yourself.
Because we are human, we goof up from time to time. The faster we learn to laugh when surprises happens, the faster we recover, find our balance, and move forward feeling better about ourselves.

2. Find your core values.
At least your top three. Core values are the ways "you do you" in the world. They're how you show up all the time in situations, without thinking about it. When you know your core values by heart, you can align everything you say, do, think, and feel. When you are fully aligned, well... you're unstoppable.

3. Know the difference between suffering and pain—and then let go of suffering.
Pain is the physical response that keeps us from doing stupid things like cutting off our noses or toes for fashion. Suffering is the story we *tell* ourselves about whatever is causing us pain. Get to know the difference. Pain is usually tolerable, but the tiniest bit of suffering amplifies pain into unimaginable torment. When you let go of suffering you can survive pain with your sense of self intact and with a deeper connection to your own strengths, abilities, and courage.

4. Surf the wave of emotion.
At a basic level, all emotions are chemistry and each one

lasts only 90 seconds in the body. The wave of chemistry floods our physical system as a response to external stimuli. You experience a wave that grows, crests and ebbs if you let it. When you allow each emotion fully and breathe through the 90-second flood, the emotion completes the cycle and dissipates. When you try to hold back uncomfortable emotions, you increase your discomfort and prolong the experience. Breathe deeply through strong emotions, allowing them to ebb naturally. Eventually, the cocktail of chemicals dissipates along with the physical experience, and your body and mind return to a state of calm.

5. Be playful.

Playfulness and creativity go hand-in-hand. When you're playful you see more options. Creativity is built on allowing yourself to "play" with ideas. The more options you allow the more resilient you become.

6. Get physical.

Moving your body increases blood flow which leads to better all-around functioning. The more you move, the better your entire system works and the better you become at "bouncing back" when life hits you with the unexpected. Dance around your house, run, bike, sled, skid, cartwheel, or whatever else bakes your cookies or jingles your bells—get outside, get moving and do it on a regular basis.

7. Make something new.

You're creative! I know some of you want to argue about this, but as a human, you're necessarily a creative animal. Creativity means thinking new thoughts, seeing different options, following divergent paths, laughing when someone else frowns, and dancing when others remain seated. Being creative allows you to dress differently whenever you choose.

It drives you to crave new tastes and helps problem-solve. Whether you can draw a turtle or a flowerpot is irrelevant, notice what you do every day that is different and do more different things. That is, by definition, creativity in action.

8. Rest.

Get enough rest. That doesn't have to mean sleeping eight hours. If you're eating super-healthy, exercising regularly, and engaged in interesting activities you may find yourself needing far fewer hours of rest. If you're bored, hungry, sad, or recovering from stress you may crave more. Listen to your body. Sleep is when you shut everything down, rest can mean sitting or relaxing quietly with a book, meditating, watching birds, or even lying on your lawn looking up at the clouds for 30 minutes. Rest can take place in short spurts or long stretches. Pay more attention to what your body craves, you'll notice when it calls for rest or really needs sleep.

9. Eat real food.

There are enough books written about this that you can search and fill your library with tons of information. I'm giving you the basics; you can spend as much or as little time researching the "why this is a great idea" elsewhere. Here goes: eat more whole, natural and organic foods. Stay away from as much packaged, "prepared," "pre-sliced," "handy" food as you can. Shop the outer edges of supermarkets for fresh items. By from local farmers' markets when possible; better yet—start a garden plot to put in your front or back yard, terrace, roof, or window. Cook things for less time to preserve nutrients and flavor. Experiment with new herbs and spices. Don't do other activities while eating—savor the flavors. Last but not least, take time to notice and appreciate what you're eating as you take each bite.

10. Thank yourself daily.

This can be the hardest one for many of us. Choose one thing each day that you did well and thank yourself out loud for it.

Whatever we appreciate, appreciates.

When we appreciate, acknowledge, and remind ourselves of what we do well, we increase our confidence, sense of self-worth, and our compassion for ourselves and others. When our compassion centers get filled, the warmth spills out to others and we become more generous and more thoughtful. It may surprise you, but appreciating your own worth also builds trust in yourself and your decisions.

In appreciating your accomplishments, you're BE-ing appreciative and that spreads appreciation to others who then spread it to their friends and their friends and their friends and so on and so on. When you acknowledge your wisdom, thoroughness, beauty, delight, thoughtfulness, actions, etc..., you help create a world built on a foundation of acknowledgment and good stuff.

These practices work because they allow us to feel supported, acknowledged, and cared for. When we experience those sensations, we can't help but be more resilient.

You Can't Avoid Death

Not to be a downer but we're all headed there.

From the moment we're born we are dying, and it's not something we can control.

Though we seem to think we can.

Plastic surgery, Botox and "youthful" hairstyles, diet, and exercise all have their effects but we can't avoid aging, and what we are really concerned about isn't aging, it's dying and death.

Trying to cheat death is a no-win situation.

The fact is that we can't not die.

We ought to at least try to embrace the process.

Make friends with it, so to speak.

Why not?

There's nothing to escape—only the process of living.

Living into the future is what we humans do best.

In fact, we are really fucking good at living forward.

The proof is in how hard we work to acquire so many things before we die. Life can feel like a form of "whoever has the most toys at the end wins." We can pretend we're winning as we accumulate objects like houses, cars, and toys. But that's aiming in the wrong direction. Having more toys can seem like success or wealth. We feel we're "doing life right," but being human really means we desire to expand. When we start thinking that expansion means *having* more rather than *being* more, we're walking towards a dead-end (pun intended).

What can you do?

Start by having more experiences, not more stuff. What humans really, really want, what we really, really want, way deep down in the messy dark corners of our psyches, is to expand into something bigger than we are at the moment. That's not more stuff... that's expanding our Self. This is way more fun and interesting in the long run of life than acquiring another shiny, new toy. It also lasts longer, and won't rust or lose all the tiny-knubbly parts that you inevitably step on barefoot.

How do I do this expanding thing?
Glad you asked!

Tip 1:
Stop accumulating objects. That shiny new car won't get you there that much better than an older model. The bigger house requires you buy more furniture, and how many rooms do you really use every day? Do you live in your house or do you live in the idea of what it represents?

Tip 2:

Start accumulating experiences.

It's what we are all here to do, anyway.

Experiences enrich life far more than things do.

Still not sure?

Quick! Do this without thinking too much about it.

Make a list of the top ten things that *really* make you happy.

Do it now!

Before you get sidetracked. Before your day gets rolling into work and responsibilities.

As fast as you can, write down the ten items that make you smile, laugh or feel contented at the end of the day.

My bet is you listed more experiences than objects.

Am I right?

If this is the case, what are you doing collecting things, when you could be out gathering experiences?

Living life is not about cheating or avoiding death at all costs. On most levels, it's got nothing to do with death. None of us will avoid dying. I invite you to revel in the juicy, rich, delicious life you have by exploring and amassing as many wonderful, amazing, terrible, exhilarating, yucky, sticky, delightful, and sweetly messy experiences as you possibly can before you kick it.

Life is messy.

It's supposed to be messy. Experiences will allow you to be messy and hopeful and resilient and to feel ALIVE! A good life can be messy like eating a super-ripe mango. Give yourself wholly to the sticky-sweet slippery process. Try to eat it before it's ripe enough and your whole mouth puckers at the tart dryness. Wait too long and it rots from the inside. *Which BTW is a perfect metaphor for what happens to us when we hold ourselves back from the richness life offers every day.*

Dive fully into the glorious dripping ripeness of life.

Live equally into the awful and the awfully wonderful events and emotions that fill your life from start to end.

Embrace that you only have a limited time in this body and you really don't know what comes next. You can imagine what might happen when you die. You can tell yourself all sorts of stories about afterlives, heavens, reincarnation, or that you'll revert to ash and soil, but most of us don't have a remembered experience of death until the pointed moment of our death, and then it's likely too late to try to describe what's going on.

By embracing the fact of death you let yourself off the hook for having to feel a certain way about it. Death is simply a part of life. Nothing more, nothing less. You can view it as the end or you can view it as one of the bookends, along with birth, that define life.

We are born with an inhale. We die with an exhale.

Life is thus one single, expansive and miraculous breath.

Tips

♦ *If you don't know of or like mangos, you can substitute persimmons, peaches, or pears for a similar grippingly sweet experience.*

♦ *If you're one of those rare persons who've had a near-death or death experience, then you'll already have a different perspective on all this. If that's you, I'd love to hear about it! Check the links at the back of the book and e-mail me your experience and take on what's what. Who knows? Your story could be included in the next book!*

Grief

Grief is one of those "biggie" emotions that, weirdly, we never really talk about.

Okay, maybe not so weird.

It can be one of the harder emotions to deal with and it's one that we in America have lost most of our cultural rituals around.

It's also the one emotion that we each experience very, *very* differently.

Let's face it, joy, fear, anger, happiness, sadness... We can imagine (at least to some degree) how any given person in our own culture may experience those. We might not get the degree right, or understand the trigger, but we can read each of those emotions fairly easily. And for ourselves, most of us can tell, whether we're in the beginning, middle or end stage.

But grief?

Grief is a whole different cocktail of emotions. There's often something bittersweet in the mix.

Grief can weave together sadness, anger, hurt, loss, loneliness, love, sweetness, and grace into one huge overwhelming experience. Because each of us will feel a different mix, it's often harder to gauge how someone else is feeling their grief. Combine this with our lack of rituals around it and we've got a potent mix of emotions, the course of which is hard to explain and harder still to understand.

Let's look at what grief is and then how best to move through it. By deepening our understanding, we'll be better prepared to help others when our nearest and dearest are mid-experience.

At its root, grief is what we experience when we face the loss of an imagined future. On a very basic level, we live life expecting that tomorrow will be pretty much the same as today. It might be a little better, a little worse, but essentially we don't actively expect much is gonna change between now and tomorrow morning... until it does.

We may know on an intellectual level that everything changes, but when we really come up against the loss of an object (like a treasured photo), an idea or plan (our dream house), or the loss of a relationship or death of someone we love, it catches us unprepared and can send us reeling. Age usually doesn't make a damn bit of difference either. No matter how old we become, the losses can knock us sideways. No one outside ourselves can really know what our experience is. We can talk about the loss and speak about our sadness, but there is always a part of us that goes through the process with one foot in the community and another in our very own, very private process.

"Surrendering to your sorrow has the power to heal the deepest of wounds...We experience conflicts, loved ones

die or suffer, dreams never manifest, illnesses occur, relationships break up and there are unexpected natural disasters. It is so important to have ways to release those pains to keep clearing ourselves. Hanging on to old pain just makes it grow until it smothers our creativity, our joy and our ability to connect with others."
~Sobonfu Somé, author

In order to heal we need to allow ourselves to move through the process. Grieving takes time, energy, and a willingness to be in the pain of growth. Growth occurs as we move from what we imagined would be into what really is. Like stepping from here to there, the process can be supported by friends, family, and ourselves, allowing rather than ignor-ing or pushing us through the process.

Loss is painful.

There's no way around that. Sometimes the loss is mild, like dropping your ice cream cone, a loss that means much less to most adults than it does to a four-year-old. Sometimes the loss feels gigantic, as in the loss of a loved one. Both losses create pain in us and we add suffering to the mix until an immense wave of emotional response crashes internally.

Step into and allow the pain as your first step. Acknow-ledge your emotions. Honestly, you don't have a choice in this. You can pretend that the loss hasn't happened or that grief is not there, but sooner or later it's going to come back to bite you in the ass. The harder you try to put it off, the sharper the bite will be.

Next, separate pain from suffering. The pain is real, the loss is real, but suffering is what we imagine the pain and loss says *about us or about our life*. Suffering is the story we tell ourselves about what the pain means. Suffering compounds pain. When we untwine the two, like untying knots from a ball of yarn, we see a clearer path forward. By clearing the way, we allow the healing that grieving provides.

Not sure of the difference between suffering and pain? Here are a few examples:

- You smash your fingers in a car door—OUCH! The physical pain is real. The suffering arrives afterward as you think about how shocking it was, how it ruined your day, or how you need to ask for help getting home.

- You meet someone amazing and start dating. After a month or two, let's say you catch them lying to you. Again, the pain is real but the suffering steps in as you get sucked into trying to figure out all the "whys" and what you imagine it says about you. Suffering comes from how we *think* about the painful event, not the pain itself.

- A loved one dies. The emotional pain is just as real as the physical pain of those smashed fingers. Suffering arrives as we lump together all the imagined futures we desired with that person that now won't happen.

It bears repeating.

Suffering is how we *think* about the loss. Pain is the physical or emotional response to a particular event. As you practice separating your pain from your suffering, you'll begin to notice that pain in every form becomes easier to cope with (yes, even physical pain).

Don't get me wrong, I'm not saying it won't hurt at all if you give up suffering. It will hurt less and for a shorter period of time. Pain without suffering will no longer co-opt your life. You can deal with pain, maybe not quite "making friends" with it, but you can handle most pain. What humans suck at handling is suffering. *Ironic, because we are amazingly good at creating suffering in so many ways, for ourselves.*

The final step is giving yourself permission to grieve. Yes, in the beginning you'll feel shitty and sad and maybe overwhelmed. You may feel like it's never going to get better. The key is to allow yourself plenty of time and space to feel the loss, breathe through it, and intentionally bring your awareness back to the present moment. Do this again and again until you're most aware of the present and everything before this particular moment fades or starts to fade into the background.

Four Simple Tips for working with Grief

♦ Set a timer for five or ten minutes and allow yourself this time and *only this amount of time* to bawl your heart out. Did it? Good! Now go wash your face, take a couple of deep breaths and get back to what you need to deal with. You can repeat this several times a day but stick to the timed approach as best you can. Having a set amount of time allows you to process the loss at different levels and practice shifting back to the present. You're teaching yourself that you can handle the pain of the loss and move yourself back into calm. Try different amounts of time between five and twenty minutes and see how you feel. Do what works best for you.

♦ Journal. *Yes! I know... everyone suggests this...* Because it works! Spending as little as five minutes journaling at the beginning of the day can help you realign and feel more grounded, productive, and happier. Take a few minutes with that first cup of coffee and write down three random things that make you smile. They can be teeny-tiny things like your dog being silly, or the sun shining through the window. They can be big scrumptious delights like the fact that you woke up today, or that you finished a big project or got thanked by someone. Make a point of saying each out loud as you write it down. The power is in acknowledging that good things still exist in your life. It's helpful to remind yourself of this even when there is pain and loss.

♦ Be clear with others about what you're experiencing. When you invite others into understanding where you are in the process, you help yourself heal. Communicating how and what you're feeling will invite more helpful support and let others know what you need. Bottling your feelings is the opposite of helpful and will extend the process instead of shortening it.

♦ Ditch anyone who tells you that you "need to stop grieving." Seriously! No one else is you. Nobody is going to grieve the same way or for the same amount of time. If someone else can't deal with your process, boot them either temporarily or permanently out of your life, get on with your grief and deal with that person, if you choose to do so, at a later time.

Tip

♦ *Please note that here I'm not talking about chronic physical pain. That is a whole different ball of wax and because it has specific ramifications for health and wellness, chronic pain in any form requires a specialized approach to help mitigate the aspects of mental and physical suffering and pain which are deeply intertwined. If you are experiencing chronic physical, mental or emotional pain, please connect with a trained practitioner to get help.*

When Doubt Crashes Life's Party

Yesterday I was thunderstruck.

That's the word for it exactly, though there was no actual thunder.

All I wanted to do was crawl back into bed and burrow deeply under the covers as though rain was pouring down in torrents outside my windows. When I closed my eyes, I could hear it rumbling and thundering across my tin roof, I could feel the pressure of that rain, heavy and thick, weighing down my heart and making my mind dull and leaden—except there was no rain.

I was having one of those days where the sinking feeling rolled over my head just about the time my coffee was ready in the morning and I was glad of having a machine that made three cups at a time.

You know the feeling, right? We all have these days. When despite the sunshine clearly visible through the windows, it feels like the world has gone grey and fallen into a kind of lusterless fog.

It's a place I know I can get stuck in if I don't start paying attention fast.

What is the heaviness that slags me down? What's this blanket of grey sogginess that I awoke underneath? What sticks me fast and holds me tightly in its gluey grip this morning? It's called doubt.

Doubt...

It's a short word filled with a thousand years' worth of stickiness.

Doubt can feel like a too-deep well, or a too-big ocean, or too much darkness. However, we experience it, it can stop us cold in a stand-still. As Isaac Newton stated, "a body in stasis will remain unmoving until an external force acts upon it."

Another version comes from the Bhagavad Gita where the prince Arjuna is so immobilized by doubt that he "sank down into the chariot and dropped his arrows and bow, his mind heavy with grief."

That pretty much summed up my morning and... we've all been there, right?

Doubt holds us fast, stuck as it were, to the bottom of our chariot, unable to choose what to do. Doubt is defined in several traditions as "a thought that touches both sides of a dilemma at the same time." So we get stuck in-between.

But the bills have to get paid, the work completed, the kids off to school, pets walked, all those things that pull on us to keep going. To pick ourselves up off the floor of our own chariot and start again.

Because that's what it felt like—starting again.

And I managed to do it. Not easy, but simple.

Simple was the only way I was going to get through yesterday.

Soooo... here's what works for me (and I offer it as a template for you) when these days roll through your life. They are simple techniques and I swear they can work miracles!

5 Steps to Action

1. Ground your feet hip-width apart and stretch your arms upward. Breath in deeply. Oxygen helps break up the torpor.

2. Grab a pad, pen, and a cup of coffee/tea and make a list of no more than 3 things you truly need to do before noon.

3. Take a cool or cold shower—seriously! Wake yourself up with soap and water in some form.

4. Put on fresh clothes (doubt often cloaks itself in yesterday's shirts and socks).

5. Scan your to-do list, choose your first task, and if you haven't already done so write the first three physical actions you need to take to move towards completion of that task, then say out loud, "ready, set, go!" and dive into your first action step. Repeat as necessary. *Trust me— this works!*

Taking immediate and appropriate action breaks up doubt the same way the warm air cracks open icebergs.

The good news is that ANY physical action can help you get rolling again. It doesn't have to be a big action. Positive Psychology tells us that Kaizen, or continuous improvement by taking small action steps, can create better and more sustainable change than big leaps.

The next time doubt sticks you to the floor of your chariot—don't worry about winning the race, start by lifting your feet, taking up the reins, and urging the horses into a trot.

Apology Accepted

It's nothing new.

We've all done things to apologize for. From careless comments to unwelcome advice or thoughtless action, each of us has at some point felt a need or desire to apologize.

This happened to me recently. I said something off the cuff, *as I often do*, and found out later that it wasn't taken the way I assumed it would be, the way it had been offered. So I tried to apologize. I fully meant it. I wanted my apology to communicate my contrition and understanding of my faux pas. Only it didn't go that way. The person (who then waved me off) would not let me apologize. He literally would not let me finish the sentence that began, "I am so sorry that I—" BAM! I was cut off mid-apology with a wave of the hand and a peremptory comment that I shouldn't continue.

Except that I felt that I should. I was embarrassed by my

behavior, willing to own what I'd done, and wanting him to know that he was right to point it out and that I'd pay more attention in the future.

I was at a retreat at the time and so I headed out for my assignment to meditate in the woods. I had a solid four-hour think on what had just happened.

What finally occurred to me is that apologies require two points of connection in order to feel complete. The first is that someone apologizes and really owns the behavior they brought. What I'd never thought about was that we hope our apology is accepted and that helps us complete the action. I don't mean the person who was wronged needs to agree and say, "Oh, that's okay." I mean that in order for an apology to fulfill its purpose, it has to be *heard*. It needs to be stated and listened to. When it's not, there's this really uncomfortable energy that hangs around and leaves everyone involved feeling dissatisfied and unbalanced.

If you are the recipient of an apology, give the gift of an honest response. Make sure you include the whole gift— the opportunity for the other person to apologize as fully as they are able. Do this and you'll make the interaction more compassionate and complete.

How to Accept a Compliment

A compliment is a gift.

It's not something that you asked for, not a gift that you hoped would show up someday like a pony, that perfect sofa, or the whole next season of your fave binge TV series.

A compliment is a gift from one person to another.

It can be the best kind of gift, the one given for no reason.

Nothing asked for or expected in return.

The woman next to you in the coffee-shop line who tells you how nice your jacket looks, or how cool your backpack is. The guy on the metro who notices your smile or what cap you've worn. The moment they speak up and offer a compliment, they are giving you a gift. Accept it.

You owe nothing at that moment.

Accepting a compliment means you've accepted the gift for what it is. Something nice. Something simple. Something easy.

Welcoming the gift allows you to open your heart. It fills you up about 75%... It fills the giver up more than 110%.

Ever notice what happens when you give a gift? You feel toasty and sparkly inside... because giving fills our hearts with love, compassion, empathy, and real warmth.

Don't run down compliments.

When someone gives you a compliment, no matter what it's for, accept it.

Be gracious.

Be welcoming.

Don't argue or brush it off as though it's some annoying insect that just landed on your shoulder.

Say "Thanks."

Nod, smile, look happy.

You just got a gift.

Out of the blue.

An unexpected surprise.

A small nicety.

Be happy.

Be generous with yourself.

Take it in, allow it to be true, *and see what happens when you see yourself as others see you.*

The real gift of a compliment is that it allows us a glimpse into how we shine our brightness and humanity in the world.

Compliments, especially from strangers, are mirrors for our souls. Accepting them clears the dust off, and sparkles them right up. The more you accept, the shinier they become.

How to Feel Confident

Self-confidence is a myth.

Take a look at any Google image search for the word "confident" and you'll see a whole bunch of truly UN-inspiring pictures of people looking surprisingly unemotional, directly into the camera.

I wonder why that is?

It can't be that feeling confident is such an unemotional state, can it?

Maybe it's that we've conflated feeling confident with power.

That's where we've gone wrong.

"Missed the boat," so to speak...

Confidence holds power and feels like elation.

It feels like floating way above the tree line and being able to see everything coming on the horizon.

Confidence feels like you have it all at your fingertips and are giddy with the joy of your position, and not needing to prove it at all.

Confidence is NOT believing in yourself.

Confidence is loving *who* you are...

How you are...

Where you are...

AS YOU ARE!

Want to feel confident more often?

Take 60 full seconds to thank yourself for something you did today.

OR

Spend two minutes naming out loud ten things you did that you're truly grateful for.

OR

Carve out a minute and a half to notice something going on around you that you normally don't bother paying attention to. Name it, acknowledge it and then see how it amplifies something already happening in your life. Notice how it relates to your existence.

Feeling confident is not something you create or manufacture or "try to work on."

Confidence is something that you ALLOW. What does "allowing it" mean to you?

Don't wait! Start today!

Don't ask "why."

Why is a rabbit hole.

It drags you into the past and keeps you stuck there.

Why is the hook that keeps you from moving forward.

Why will drain your energy.

Why is a stalling tactic.

Asking *why* something happened (is happening, will happen...) is a surefire way to be immediately convinced that you need to do a million other things before taking action.

Why is the biggest excuse in the world.

Why is procrastination in three letters.

It's sneaky, it seems so small and innocuous, like that first single ant at a picnic—one shows up and the rest follow to eat your BBQ.

Wondering *why* brings the action to a halt. WHY does not matter (most of the time).

I promise you–stop asking WHY and:

- You'll figure out everything you need to know in the process of taking action and you'll feel more confident because you'll have more options and answers.

- The necessary answers will come into view as you move forward and this boosts confidence.

- Answers surface amidst action. The more action steps you take, the more you build confidence.

- Seeing options and answers adds to your flow instead of stalling it. When you are in FLOW, you get more accomplished and accomplishments acknowledged lead to... you guessed it, more confidence.

Next Time...

The next time you find yourself stuck... on anything, take three deep breaths through your nose. Ask yourself, "What is the next <u>physical</u> action I need to take?" Complete that step, check your progress, and take the next step and the next, and so on.

Celebrate each step as well as the final outcome being reached.

No Time for Panic

Whatever is happening in your life right this minute, I can promise you this is not the time to panic.

I know, you probably want to argue with me about why it is, in fact, the perfect time to panic. Why you really ought to pull a hat over your head, wave your hands in the air and rush into the street warning everyone that the world is going to hell... that we've already passed the gates and are descending into Dante's fifth ring and, why the heck can't I see that it's only going to get worse?

Seriously! Take the hat off your head because it's 80° Fahrenheit outside right now and you'll overheat. Here, I made some blueberry muffins. Have one. There's fresh coffee too, and chamomile tea. Here's a plate, napkin, some butter and jam. Now go sit your arse down and eat while I let you in on a not very secret secret...

Panicking only makes it worse.

Whatever "IT" is, I promise you, panicking is the best way to make it twice as bad twice as fast. So let's slow the roll, sip something delicious, have another muffin and look at what we can do to make things better right away.

True story (and you can ask my friend Heather about this because we were sharing a house at the time):

One Saturday morning in early November 2019, I woke up at my normal way-the-fuck-too-early-for-a-weekend hour of 5:00 a.m. and went downstairs to start the coffee while the heater warmed up my "office/meditation/yoga/where-the-cat-thinks-everything-is-for-her-to-laze-about-on" room. Heather was sleeping in peaceful ignorance and the dog snored away on the dog bed. Nothing looked out of place—but as I made coffee, something felt off. I walked around the kitchen, noting that I must've taken my phone up to bed with me. No phones on the counter. Weird. I walked around some more. No backpacks on the floor near the sofa and—ah-ha! My car keys were missing. In fact, pretty much everything that might have been grab-able and seemed to have value... was gone. I walked around again checking doors and saw that the garage door was open. I knew that wasn't right and then it hit me. My bright red car was not in the driveway. My car had been stolen! Holy shit! What the fuck? How did they break in, steal this stuff and the dog never made a peep? It was not yet 6:00 a.m. on a Saturday so... which neighbor was I going to go wake up to call the police for me? Remember, cell phones... gone.

I went back inside, coffeepot gurgling like nothing was awry, though it all felt pretty surreal to me. Heading upstairs, still trying to be quiet when I realized: *Well, that's stupid because I'm about to wake up Heather and tell her we got robbed and my car is missing.* The good news? Her car was still parked in front of the house. I tapped on Heather's door, woke her out of a sound sleep with the calmest words I could manage: "Hey Heather, we got robbed, nothing's broken but I've gotta run next door to call the cops." She blinked at me a few times because, seriously, who gets woken up like this on a Saturday? Then she rubbed her eyes and said the magic words, "Wait, I have my work phone up here."

With that simple sentence, I could feel millions of jittering nerves give up their frenetic internal dance with a happy little sigh. "We can get help!" My brain whooped with delight and started its own happy dance inside my head. My heart stopped racing itself. We had a phone! We didn't have to wake the neighbors! There was coffee! Small things, people... small things make the world a better place even when you've been robbed.

I dialed the cops and Heather tore herself from sleep and did all the things you do in the morning after a really fun and really late Friday night. Authorities notified. Next task—cancel credit cards. That took all of four minutes online and still the police hadn't magically shown up... so I made banana bread.

Now, let's stop and think about why this is actually one of the most sensible things to do if first thing in the morning you discover that you've been robbed.

First, you already reported the crime. Second, credit cards are nixed and there's nothing you can do about the car right now. Third—you've already got coffee made and there might as well be something tasty to go with it, riiiiight? And fourth, your mama always told you to eat breakfast. Right! So, banana bread because there are always ripe bananas somewhere, they're good for you and the bread takes exactly eight minutes to mix and 20 minutes to bake.

While it baked, I sipped my cup of java and made a list of everything that'd been stolen, starting with my bright red, almost new car. (Did I mention that I drive a stick shift? That's important later...)

Heather arrived in the kitchen in time to be handed her

phone, a mug of coffee, and a slice of still-too-hot-to-eat banana bread and starts canceling credit cards and making her list of missing items. By the time the cops show up, we've talked with the neighbors, many of whom had their cars rifled through, and miscellaneous items taken. Heather and I are refilling our mugs and starting in on a second helping of bread.

Heather told me later she was pretty sure the cop didn't actually believe we'd been robbed. We were too calm. Evidently, it threw him off so much that he never even dusted for prints (but that's another thing altogether). Anyway, turns out that the robbers got in through a door that we normally kept locked. They swept the first floor for stuff they could grab and were gone in something like four minutes with my car. Next, they scavenged through every car and porch on our street and dumped everything they could grab into my vehicle, which became hodgepodge central.

Let me digress to say that when I write, "they grabbed everything," I mean they grabbed stuff that made no sense... outdoor cushions, random coins, bottles of sunblock, hand lotion, more pens than my father ever collected, all manner of sunglasses and batteries, and all the random-ass stuff we leave in our cars and on our porches. My VW became the storage unit for the haul and by the time the thieves were nabbed a few hours later, my VW was filled with a massive amount of junk.

The stupid/funny part was that they were caught lurching down the street in front of my neighbor who happened to be on the phone with a policewoman at that exact moment. She was reporting her own missing items when the bandits blundered by. I say lurched because evidently, they couldn't figure out how to work the clutch and they were driving in fits and starts down the street.

My neighbor yelled, "STOP!" and told the cops what was

happening. The bandits were caught shortly afterward, sitting in a parking lot with bags of hoagie rolls, McDonald's food, and the rest of their haul. It was so opposite of what we see on TV police shows when the cops asked us, "Can you call your neighbors, have them come down here and go through all this so we don't have to tag it?"

In the end, we got back almost everything—though I was pissed about the brand-new lipstick in the perfect shade of red. After a good scrubbing, and burning of various herbs, my car was restored. Two weeks later another neighbor called to say he'd found my sunglasses along with several other pairs under the back seat of his car... go figure!

What can we learn about building resilience from this whole incident? Being resilient didn't keep me from being robbed or having to sanitize my car that afternoon. It didn't keep us from the headaches that accompany having your stuff taken from your house—including the phone which as we all know these days is akin to stealing someone's entire working memory.

What resilience did was allowed me to stay calm, feel okay and not have my day totally ruined. It helped me prioritize what needed to happen and how I could best deal with the emerging situation. It helped me cope without too much fuss. Most important of all, it allowed me to be helpful to others as the robber's antics unfolded, and not feel a gigantic backlash of emotions after the incident.

Why is that a key part of all this?

People who feel unsupported and scared are more likely to have a trauma response than people who feel they're in control of a situation. Even to a small extent. We humans like to feel that we've got things handled. The more in-line that feeling is with events taking place around us, the calmer and less stressed we feel. Our bodies, which happen to include our brains, respond to stress in various ways. One way we have of lessening stressful effects is to take steps and feel in control (and this is important) in *ways that align with the reality of our current situation.*

One way to lessen the effects of stress is to take steps and feel in control in ways that align with the reality of the current situation.

The whole thing could've gone very differently if we'd panicked. Let's imagine that I woke up, found the house had been robbed, the car stolen, and started shouting my head off and running around waving my hands in the air. The first thing that would happen is that my body would have released a whole slew of stress hormones and triggered my Sympathetic Nervous System (SNS). Let me tell you, that system is anything but sympathetic! It's what makes your heart leap to your throat, tears spring to your eyes, your breathing gets shallow and essentially you suffocate yourself which triggers even more feelings of panic, worry, more stress, and way, way less clear-minded thinking.

Had my SNS been driving the bus when the cops arrived, I'd have babbled a whole bunch, had a hard time recalling what might've been stolen, not been able to answer their questions or give them a clear list of what and where and when. We all would've been fumbling for a good 30 to 60 minutes just to get the basic information, which would've meant that my neighbor would *not* have been looking for my car... and so on.

By leaning heavily into resilience, the whole situation resolved faster, and with a better outcome than would've been likely had it dragged out through panicked action. Being resilient and taking necessary actions also kept my body in a state that my old karate teacher calls ready-relaxed. This means being totally ready for whatever comes at you while remaining so relaxed that you could pull a Matrix-like shift and sidestep the whole thing. No hit, little impact and you keep moving.

Ready-relaxed is the equivalent of telling your brain that everything is copasetic and that you are ready for whatever shows up. It's a state of resilience where you give your entire body the message that you're okay and taking action. Here's the key: your body (yes, including your brain) likes action. By choosing actions that bring you closer to your desired outcome, your whole system chills out and you bypass frantic, non-productive, and even harmful behavior.

Ready-relaxed is resilience in action.

Panic is the opposite.

Below are some quick, practical moves you can make when something throws you off-kilter and you feel a tidal wave of panic sweep through your body.

♦ *The first is to breathe. I know... Everyone and their dog Eric says this, and there's a reason for that... because it fucking works. Slow, rhythmic, <u>nasal</u> breathing has been scientifically proven to positively affect the brain, heart, digestion, immune system, and even the expression of genes. Start by slowly EXHALING three times (don't worry, the inhales happen on their own). Notice how you feel. Rinse and repeat as necessary to clear your head and stop you reacting right this second.*

♦ *Take your right hand and make the "Girl Scout" sign with your first two fingers together. Turn your left palm upwards and place your extended right fingers into the center of your palm making firm, little circles. Count to ten. Repeat as necessary to relieve tension. This is acupressure. In the center of your palms are adrenal points and even western science understands that panic induces a rush of adrenaline. By gently and firmly massaging this point, you can reduce the level of adrenaline in your body, thus reducing the feeling of panic.*

♦ *Grab a notepad and jot down the outcome you most want. For example: "I want my stolen items back and to not have it take all day." By naming the outcome you want and taking a pause between reacting to whatever is happening, and the action you take, you aim yourself directly at what you want to create next.*

♦ *The last comes from my Russian great-grandmother, "No matter what happens, go make a sandwich, and make mine tuna with celery." Which, if you think about it is just 'effing sensible, because we all think better when we've had a nosh.*

If you've put any or all of these tips into play you'll find yourself feeling more in control, calmer, and will have increased your resilience. All lead to long-term benefits and general well-being, so go ahead, give 'em a try when anything, and I do mean anything, startles you into panic mode.

Tip

♦ *These moves also help you buy time by creating a pause between reaction and taking action. This is always benefi-cial when things go haywire.*

Don't Be Bored

"I'm borrrrred!"

Whether you know it or not, this is one of the most dangerous statements you can make.

Why?

Because it means you have given up your power over your own life.

Hunh? Seriously?

How can that be when all I'm saying is that *"I'm bored that there's nothing to do?"*

Knock that shit off. There is *always* something to do.

You just haven't thought about it. Or gotten curious enough yet.

Or you're waiting for someone else to make the first move, or come up with the idea.

Or you haven't decided what you want.

Being bored means you aren't looking around.

The universe is big, there's lots to play with, tons to be curious about.

Something new is happening every single second, even inside your own body.

Just think about that for a full minute and see if you stay bored.

Really... think about it... Be genuinely curious.

When we are curious about the world, about ourselves, we don't get bored.

Being bored boils down to being boring. Are you boring?

Probably not.

You're avoiding a situation or choice.

Or something that you didn't expect has happened.

Or something you expected to happen, didn't.

Whatever your particular situation, feeling bored really means that you haven't dived into the question "What do I want to create next for myself?"

What *do* you want next?

What do you need to do to create it?

Whether it's a swim on a hot day, a date with someone, or a new direction for your company or product, start by seeing what you're aiming for and then be curious about what you need to do next.

Being curious about #AllTheThings all the time guarantees you'll never be bored again.

Tips

♦ *Find yourself low on energy? Drink some water first. Often we are dehydrated and that can affect our ability to think and feel motivated.*

♦ *Feeling bored because there's nothing to do? Off the top of your head, list five things that make you laugh out loud. Now go do one of them.*

♦ *Boredom due to frustration at a situation? Write down the five things you might be able to do to change the way things are (even a little). Remember: You're 100% responsible for how you feel and 50% able to take action to change things.*

About Meditations

Let's get a few things straight about meditation.

Meditation is a serious thought or study of a single object or topic. It's all about being aware and present in this moment... *not that one... this moment... look, stay in this moment with me... this one... right here... right now... Challenging right?*

Meditation doesn't *always* mean sitting, or saying "Auummm..." with your eyes closed for an hour.

Meditation isn't how it looks in the pictures with everything serene and peaceful.

Meditation isn't religious, it doesn't care who you are or what you believe.

Meditation doesn't require you to wear, eat or think anything special.

Meditation likes you just as you are, however you are, right this moment.

The truth is that there are hundreds of different systems and styles of mediation. Each one offers a different set-up or set of ideas and each one will feel different to each of us.

So how do you find what works for you?

The first step is to understand what the purpose of mediation is.

Ready...?

All meditation is aimed at focusing your mind on one thing, intentionally, without judgment.

Whether you sit, stand, walk, do the dishes, put on your socks or go get take-out, the thing you're really working on is focusing your mind completely on that one thing and only that one thing.

It does <u>not</u> matter what the one thing is. Some things are more challenging to our ability to focus. It's often easier to sit quietly and focus on your breath than it is to walk through the woods and remain fully focused on your breathing, your footsteps, or the feel of the air on your cheek. Washing dishes or raking leaves might feel more accessible as they are repetitive tasks that don't usually require a lot of thought. (Just don't drop Aunt Sarah's beloved gravy boat while meditating on the way the water swishes over each plate, cup, and spoon). Walking meditations can be fairly simple if you don't have to navigate busy city streets and lots of people. Then again, the challenge might feel like you've won the Olympics of meditation if you manage more than a block without losing focus.

The key is to be willing to train your mind to quieten and notice everything it can about one particular thing for a certain period of time. You choose the thing and the amount of time.

Try this:

♦ Two minutes of focus on slow, long nasal breathing helps trigger your parasympathetic nervous system and calms your body in general, as well as promotes a feeling of well-being.

- ♦ Double that and take four minutes to stare at the sky, day or night. Those four minutes will help you feel more balanced and grounded. As you gaze upward, let yourself be curious about what you see, without *thinking* about it.

"Training the mind in meditation is like training a puppy. We put the puppy down and say, 'Sit. Stay.' What does it do? It gets up and runs around. 'Stay.' It turns around again. Twenty times, 'Stay.' After a while, slowly, the puppy settles down. Through practice, gently and gradually we can collect ourselves and learn how to be more fully where we are. But remember, this bringing of the heart and mind to what we do builds slowly."
    ~*Jack Kornfield, author of* The Untrained Mind

There is a reason that millions of experienced meditators call it *practice*.

We don't call it "Meditation Achieved." There's a reason for that.

No matter how long or how often you "sit" you're always practicing. Every day is different and each meditation will be too! One day you wake up feeling happy, another, feeling tired or sore. Sometimes your mind feels calm, other times it's racing like a gerbil on a wheel and nothing gets done. All these situations will help you get "better" at meditating if you're willing to work with them.

Willingness is the key here. Yup! You've gotta be willing to take the three, five, fifteen, or however-many-minutes to practice. It doesn't matter how long you do it, just that you do it—and do it regularly. Practice a bit every day and you'll find yourself able to go longer and longer without really trying. *You might even start to crave longer meditation sessions!*

Our bodies like meditation. Our physical body has time to relax, repair, and regroup. Do any form of meditation and you allow your body to do what it naturally wants to do, which is to aim toward health. Even in a walking practice, you slow your thoughts and allow your body to lead the way. Your body will let you know what it needs to feel good, you simply have to get good at listening.

The great thing is that bodies (as opposed to thoughts) don't often lie. If you cut your finger you feel the flash of pain that tells you to take care of the cut. If you bump your shin, you'll feel the dull ache that continues until the tissue has healed. Bodies aim themselves toward health and minds get in the way, producing thoughts that rise into emotions and emotions that drive actions. Sometimes the actions are helpful, moving us towards health and vitality. Other times they stem from habits, beliefs, and patterns which move us into illness and stress. The choice is yours to make about which direction you follow.

Fun Fact: You can become "addicted" or habituated to feeling stressed (the result of continually elevated cortisol levels) just like being addicted to other physical experiences. When you change the behaviors that increase cortisol and stress in the body, you may notice you feel weird or not yourself. Because your Self is used to feeling stressed, and you are changing the way you are BE-ing in the world. With time, your body will re-acclimate to a more normal level of hormones and this will be your new normal.

By practicing meditation daily, you're training your mind towards ease and health. That means lower levels of stress, which means you'll think and feel better overall.

All this in less than 10 minutes a day!

Feeling adventurous? Try one of these practices.

Don't worry if your mind drifts off from time to time, that's normal. Notice when you have followed a thought and gently bring your mental focus back. You'll gain skill at holding focus as you practice.

Find a short path you can walk for at least seven to ten minutes. Woodland paths, parks, greenways, or beaches are best for this as you won't have to dodge traffic. If you're new to walking in meditation, opt for a paved or gravel path so you don't worry about roots and rocks tripping you up. As you walk, focus your mind softly and be gently curious about your surroundings. Walk slowly enough that you're able to take in everything around you. Notice trees and other plants, the path under your feet. Pay some attention to the sounds you hear, perhaps stand still for a moment to listen. Note any scents as you walk along and see if you can let go of labeling anything you notice as "good" or "bad."

No time to go outside? No worries! Set a timer for seven to ten minutes and settle yourself by a window. Place your feet hip-width or slightly wider apart, flat on the floor. Wiggle your torso upwards gently, shaking off random thoughts and physical tension. Imagine lightly touching the top of your head to the ceiling and nudge your chin back just a smidge. Now shake out your arms, wrists, and hands and let them rest loosely on your legs. Elbows softly bent; eyes open. Choose to focus on one object in front of you. It might be the rain on the windowpane, it could be something further out, a tree, flowers, grass, rain, sleet, snow, or sky. Choose one object and allow yourself to look at it as though you had never seen this particular object before and get really curious about it. Stop when your timer dings.

Feeling under the weather? Before you get out of bed, stretch your body lengthwise and then lie on your back, arms by your sides. Keep your eyes open so you don't fall back to sleep, mentally walk your attention from the top of your head, down your torso and limbs, and then back up to the top of your head. Start by focusing down the right side of your body and moving back up the left side. Do this twice slowly and then focus your attention down the middle column of your body from head to toes and back up again. As you send your attention along your body, notice what each area feels like. Be curious—do you notice tightness, achiness, or tension in some areas? Use the first pass to notice whatever is present in your body. With a second pass, slow down around any areas that feel unwell and imagine bringing light and ease to that area before continuing with the practice. Notice anything that feels different from when you began. The more slowly you practice this, the more benefits you'll experience.

Grab a quickie! When you're feeling rushed, this super-quick, three-step practice will help you remain calm under pressure.

Step 1: Stop moving.

Step 2: Exhale slowly and deeply through your nose, mouth closed.

Step 3: Inhale slowly and fully without creating tension, through your nose, mouth closed.

That's it! You can repeat as often as necessary, but simply by exhaling fully, you begin to trigger your body to relax.

When we exhale, we quiet the brain as a whole and particularly the amygdala which is responsible for our anxiety response. By starting with the exhale you'll breathe more with your diaphragm. Diaphragmatic breathing is the key to engaging your body's natural ability to lower stress. Since you started by exhaling, you'll have primed your body to inhale more diaphragmatically and less from your upper chest than if you start with the inhale.

Imagine exhaling anything that's bugging you. Allow your breath to flow inward through your nose naturally, without tension or stress. The more times you repeat the three steps the more you synchronize your heartbeat and breathing. You'll also clear your mind and create space for some new ideas and perspectives.

Tips

♦ *Be patient with yourself as you practice meditation. Just like learning to tie your shoes, this is a skill. The more you practice, even for a few minutes at a time, the better and easier it becomes to drop fully into and stay within the calming space that meditation can create.*

♦ *Starting with shorter times, say two to five minutes for the first week or two, will support a stronger long-term practice than diving into twenty to sixty minutes right from the outset.*

♦ *Sometimes our brain gets in the way as well, as with traumatic injury and phantom pain where the brain isn't correctly mapping or responding to nerve messages, or where nervous systems over/under-trigger pain responses.*

♦ *If you want more support for meditation, check out more guided meditations on the website anunstoppablelife.com.*

READER RESOURCES

Open to Compassion

A guided meditation to open and reconnect you to your own compassion center. When we are connected to this energetic center in our own energy fields, we are better able to maintain alignment with ourselves during stressful times.

Settle into your seat and allow your body to move until you find a comfortable, grounded position with your feet flat on the floor. Bring your attention to the compassion center located halfway between your heart and the base of your throat.

Notice a clear, crystalline, pink, brilliant vibration much like a rose quartz color, very clear, very intense, but cool in temperature. Allow that simply to start to grow. It may start as a spark or it may start as a sphere or a line, the form doesn't matter.

Allow that crystalline, clear pink, vibration to expand very gently, without forcing anything. You can breathe through your mouth, through your nose, whatever works. Focus your attention on that expansion, so you're noticing the expansion as it happens rather than creating it. You may notice that it expands in a more linear form, or in a spherical form. It might be just a blob, it might be like a fog. Whatever form it expands in is perfect. Allow it to draw sideways so that it is expanding sideways from left to right, and becomes wider than your body.

You may notice there's a certain width it hits, and it's going to stay there. It may feel about a foot to a foot and a half-width, out from either side of your body to the left and the right.

Notice the width that it has expanded front and back, that might be the same, it might be a little bit less. Again, whatever it expands to is perfect. So, you're following the expansion with your intention rather than creating it. Now bring your attention to the front of that crystalline pink vibration and start to notice a very clean, thin line of vibration moving from your compassion center in your physical body outward towards the horizon.

It goes past the horizon— you can't actually see where it ends—and then it loops back towards you. So, it's doubling the energy coming back. Increasing the vibration and increasing what we can call the quantity, although that's not quite accurate, but the quantity of vibration coming back to you, allowing you to fill your own compassion center.

You may notice that the vibration within your energy field becomes a little richer.

It might feel a little more energetic and a little denser, but the color gets a little bit richer, deepening slightly as it fills. As the compassion center within your own energy body fills it begins to spill outward in a funnel from the front of your body.

Notice that you can direct this funnel to be narrow or wide.

You can choose to funnel this excess of compassion outward generally, or to a specific person, or people who would use some extra compassion right now.

Go wider still and more broadly to the very ground where you're sitting, sending it outward to any people in your neighborhood or community, to any beings in your general vicinity, or even more widely to the state, the country, the continent, the planet, however widely you want.

Notice if there's a point where it just normally or naturally feels like it's ending or trailing off, and if you feel as though it has extended a little too far, just draw it back in a little. It might feel like a little slurping of the energy back in until you feel like you've got that funnel of energy moving outward as an excess in an amount or a level that feels suitable to where your energy level is now, so not overextending yourself.

Simply notice how it feels to extend that compassion and that vibration, which is excess of what you need. Notice if there's a cooling sensation in your own physical body, a kind of settling.

Taking three or four easy and full breaths at your own pace, allow that funnel to slowly fold upon itself, coming to a very gradual and natural ending. So that you still are retaining the fullness of compassion and energy in your own body, your own energy field.

Take your time to breathe, as you come to the end of whatever feels like the right number of breaths for you, gently open your eyes.

You can download the audio of this meditation at AnUnstoppableLife.com.

Blue Spiral Vibration

Blue Spiral Vibration Guided Meditation

This meditation is great for creating an internally balanced sense of calm. It's also useful when you're building a new habit of holding your own boundaries gently. Listen to or practice this short meditation at least once a day and notice what is different after seven days.

Imagine your name like a spiral of blue vibration, different shades of blue, different densities that all vibrate together in a kind of rope or wave.

Imagine this spiral starting from far, far away and below you, spiraling up through and all around you so that you become part of the rope, part of the wave.

You're being spiraled upward as it continues. If you follow

it, you notice that it connects back to itself below you, without being able to see that connection.

You feel it there, one continuous line that connects upon itself. The spiral that connects to spiral your name through you, from your base to the top, drawing you out as though you were a long rope being wound and wound within a larger rope of vibration.

Allow yourself to unwind within the vibration, becoming less of yourself and more of yourself. Less the individual and more awareness of the connection to consciousness. Notice how it feels as you unwind your physical body, allowing it to shear away and unwrap you.

Allow the vibration of this blue rope—all the hues of blue from lightest to darkest, some matte, some shiny, all twisted into this rope and wave. Twisting and untwisting so many times, so easily and smoothly that it becomes unclear whether it is twisting together or twisting apart at any given moment. Within these turns and twists, you're held.

It's all around you and within you. Your name is drawn out until that word has very little meaning. Your name no longer means just you in this body. Can you allow that name vibration, that roping blue spiral to twist and untwist through and around you, connecting to all through infinity across the field as a loop that looks like a line?

As you feel your physical body unwinding within the spiral, through the spiral, becoming part of it, notice the inner vibrations unwinding, the inner parts of you dissolve in a dissection. Imagine yourself as this rope coming unwound, creating space within the spiral so that it's more and more difficult to tell where the parts of you are in parts of the spiral.

All seen as experienced, all seen and experienced as a vibration of blues. There is a sense of one pure hue, unnamed, unnamable. It may be that when you bring your attention to focus on it, you notice lighter and darker, some shining and sparkling, others matte and dull. The more you try to focus on any one line of vibration along this unnamable hue the more you see the spiral as a whole and experience it.

The more you allow yourself to see and experience the whole the more you see the various threads spiraling each upon themselves, through and around you and with each other to create this enormous spiraling rope, threaded, vibration, blue, your name, which is all consciousness, which is you, which is not a name, which is an unnamable. You and the vibration stretch and expand so that there is no beginning or end that you're aware of. Within this, you come back into yourself and your own physical spiral.

Start to become aware again of the difference between your physical body and the spiral vibration of energy that moves through and around you. Taking your time, allow yourself to relax back into your body, back into your breath. At your own pace, take three easy inhales and three long exhales. Come back inside your physical body and into the space you're sitting in.

You can download the audio of this meditation at AnUnstoppableLife.com.

Five-Minute
Balance Energy

A quickie meditation to balance your energy and give you a boost.

Allow yourself to sit comfortably with a straight spine and lengthen through the back of your neck so it's easy to breathe. You might shrug your shoulders around once or twice just to loosen them up, then allow your hands to rest gently on your thighs, palms up or down. Take a deep breath in and let it out with a sigh, releasing anything that is on your mind at this moment. Give yourself the next five minutes to calm and ground.

Imagine tucking your feet even more deeply into the earth. Allow your feet to be flat on the floor or on the ground.

Imagine that you've wiggled your toes even more deeply into the earth, feeling the warmth from the earth coming up through your feet, up through your legs, and into your whole pelvic area. And as you draw that warmth of the earth up into your body, imagine that it carries with it a vibration of bright green light.

You have this sense of moving upward from the center of the Earth. The warmth, the support, and the energy moving up into your body. Allow it to move upward beyond your pelvis into your belly and allow each inhale to draw that energy and warmth and green vibration further upward into your chest. Breathing it up into the top of your chest.

With the next breath, breathe it up into your throat and notice if you feel an expansion or a loosening in your throat.

Allow that warmth to come up the back of your head and imagine it filtering into the center of your entire head and expanding outward in a comforting, warm, energetic vibration. Allow that green brilliant energy to move upward and out the crown of your head, spilling down outside of your body in all directions, in all dimensions, pooling underneath your feet.

Imagine drawing more bright green energy up from the center of the Earth. Moving upward through your legs, through the center of your body, filling all the nooks and crannies in your body. Draw that green brilliant energy up your entire body. Allow it to spill down your arms and out your fingertips. You can imagine it dripping off your fingertips to be reabsorbed by the ground.

Draw the energy up through your neck and head and allow it to spill again out the top of your head in all directions, in all dimensions, pooling again into the ground. Being reabsorbed there and taking with it any obstructions and stress.

One last time imagine drawing deeply from the center of the Earth. Bring the bright green vibration and warmth up through the bottoms of your feet, up your legs into your pelvis. Imagine it gathering power there and moving upward through your belly, ribs, and chest.

Allow some of it to spill down your arms and out your fingertips, the rest of it moving upward, from your chest to your throat, then from your throat filling your entire head. Allow it to spill out the crown of your head and down all sides of your body in all dimensions. Again being reabsorbed by the earth, taking away all impurities, all obstructions.

Now, just allow yourself to reset your energy level for the day. So without thinking about it, just allow it to come to wherever feels level to you. You don't have to think about where you're setting it. Just know that if you say *I allow my energy to level out and balance*, it will do so.

Notice if you feel an opening or loosening somewhere in your body as your energy level finds its balance for the day. Bring your attention to that connection that you have with the earth through the soles of your feet.

Know that you're always fully supported by the earth and that you can draw this energy up through your body at any point during the day when you need a little boost. As you finish this meditation, take three breaths at your own pace, and slowly open your eyes.

You can download the audio of this meditation at AnUnstoppableLife.com.

Blue-Green Vibration Cleansing

A seven-minute meditation to release the old and draw in the new.

Allow yourself to fully settle into your seat. Feel free to wiggle your spine and body and then find some stillness, feeling fully supported by the chair, your cushion, or the earth.

Lengthen your spine gently upward, imagining that you could reach the top of your head towards the sky. Lengthening gently down from your sitting bones into the earth without tension. Take one or two deep cleansing breaths to let go of whatever has come before this moment in time. Allow yourself to settle into your breath and into your body fully.

With each inhale, imagine drawing the breath up from

below your feet, deep in the earth. Imagine each breath as a gentle wave of blue-green vibration as clear and pure as the clearest ocean water. Each inhale allows you to drink up this beautiful blue-green vibration.

Breath it up into your ankles. Every exhale allows you to release it back to the earth. Bring the next breath of blue-green vibration up to your knees, allowing it to gently rise and exhale it back down to the earth.

Inhale, sipping that blue-green vibration up to your hip-bones, letting it slide back down to the earth. Inhale it up to your waist, allowing your whole lower body to fill with blue-green vibration, very clear, very bright, and very cleansing. Allow it to fall back to the earth on the exhale.

Inhale blue-green vibration up into your rib cage. Imagine it expanding your rib cage in every direction, front, and back, side to side. Notice if your ribs feel that they can move a little more freely. Expanding a little more in every direction. Then allow the breath to exhale all the way back down below your feet into the earth.

Sip the next breath of vibration all the way up to your collarbones at the level of your armpits. And again, notice how your entire ribcage expands in all directions with this breath.

Without holding it at the top, allow it to exhale, slowly releasing it all the way back down. Follow its path down and out of your body as you exhale, below your feet and back to the earth.

Again, inhale gently all the way up, bringing blue-green vibration all the way up into the base of your neck and exhaling, following it all the way down to below your feet all the way into the earth.

The next vibration of breath, draw that vibration of oceanic clarity all the way up to the level of your eyes. Imagine it clearing and cleansing your sight in every dimension, on every level, before allowing it to fall back through the earth, taking with it unnecessary ideas, thoughts, and emotions.

Anything you are ready to release, allow to fall back into the earth as well for compost. With a final deep breath, draw that clear vibration all the way from the center of the Earth up through your body, up through the crown of your head, and allow it to spill out the crown of your head, falling gently down your back like rain to be absorbed by the earth.

Two more breaths like that, inhaling all the way up from the center of the Earth through your entire body. Clear blue-green vibration, clearing and cleansing up through the crown of your head, spilling out the crown of your head and down your back. Taking anything unused and unwanted away with it to be reabsorbed by the earth.

One last inhale, drawing that blue-green vibration of clarity and ease up through the bottom of your feet, through your entire body, expanding each area of the body as you breathe upward through the crown of your head, allowing it out the crown of your head to spill down your back and back into the earth.

Now releasing the breathing pattern. Sit quietly. Notice whether you need to breathe or not for the next moment or two.

At your own pace, taking your time, very gently open your eyes, and go on with the rest of your day.

You can download the audio of this meditation at AnUnstoppableLife.com.

Circle of Breath

A meditation for releasing strong emotions

Settle into your seat. If you're sitting on a chair, place your feet flat on the floor very gently but firmly. If you're sitting on a cushion or the earth, settle in and wiggle around until you find that very comfortable, almost weightless position. Allow your shoulders to shrug around a little to loosen up your spine and then find stillness in the body.

Bring your attention to your breath. Notice your breath as a cycle. A circle of in and out, in and out without pause. Without changing your breath in any particular way, simply follow the breath as a circle. You may feel it moving lower to higher or left to right. Allow your breathing to be easy. Allow your inhale to flow gently and directly into your exhale without a stutter, without holding the breath.

Let your breath flow from the inhale directly to the exhale and from the exhale directly to the inhale.

As you follow your breath with your mind, start to imagine the breath as a circle. It might be like a hula-hoop or a sphere. Whatever image comes to mind, allow it and notice if there are any areas of the breath that feel a little stuck or sticky or a little rough.

As your mind follows the breath. You might imagine it like an iron gently smoothing out any areas of roughness. No need to use a lot of pressure, a very light touch will do here.

Smoothing out the breath from the exhale, to the inhale, to the exhale without pause, notice if one side of your breath feels like it's rushing. Can you balance out your circle so that your breath becomes completely centered, so that it feels easy?

As you follow the cycle and circle of your breath, you may notice a color. The color might change as you inhale and exhale. It may shift a lot. It may shift a little. It may become clear in parts as you breathe for longer and longer. Or it may intensify as emotions come up and you breathe them out.

As your mind follows your breath, allow any thoughts that come up to be breathed out. If emotions arise, notice how the color or the texture of your breath might change while you're feeling that emotion, and then again, like the thoughts, breathe them out.

Follow the circle and cycle of your breath. Whether it's a hula-hoop or a sphere. Notice if the color has shifted now that you've been breathing for several moments. Notice if it's gotten easier. Be curious about the difference without needing to change anything intentionally.

Can you allow your breath to be truly easy and round, smooth and even, soft and easy and warm? Remember that we always have our breath with us, whether we notice it or not.

I invite you to take a few more inhale and exhale cycles at

your own pace. When you feel complete, take your own time. Then gently open your eyes and sit quietly for a few moments. I wish you well for the rest of your day.

You can download the audio of this meditation at AnUnstoppableLife.com.

Depth of Heartbeat

A meditation for reconnecting with your heart and passion

As you settle in for your meditation, allow your whole body to stretch out in every direction. Stretching your arms wide away from each other, reach them up towards the sky, intertwine your fingers and press your palms to the sky.

Lean to the right, leaning to the left, and then twisting left and right, right and left to open up your entire spine, your entire rib cage. Spiral your wrists around. If you're sitting on a chair, pick up each foot and spiral each ankle around. Notice what it feels like as you move your fingers and toes. You may start to spiral your knees around and open each of your knee joints up, stretching one foot, heel pressing away from you. Then pointing that toe. Then move to the other foot, heel pressing away from you strongly and then pointing that toe.

Repeating as feels good.

You can allow your whole pelvis to rock forward, arching your spine and sending your elbows to touch behind you. Next, roll your shoulders inward and pull your belly button towards your spine. Roll your pelvis forward again, arching your back, maybe even looking up towards the ceiling. Then allow your shoulders to rise towards your ears, rolling your shoulders forward.

Pull your belly button fully towards your spine. Gaze towards the ground on an exhale. Inhale, roll everything open again and shrug your shoulders gently around, finding some stillness in the body. Allow your hands to rest gently on your thighs, palms up or down.

Notice your breathing and then bring your attention to your heartbeat. Imagine diving inside your body. Imagine listening with every possible sense to your heartbeat.

As you listen quietly with curiosity, can you start to notice that you're hearing your heartbeat not only with your ears but with the vibration in your rib cage? Do you notice that your entire rib cage becomes a kind of vibration or drum that echoes your heartbeat?

As you listen more carefully, you may notice that you start to hear several variations. You may be aware of the right side and the left side of your heart beating independently and in tandem. That one beats and then the other follows.

Sit quietly and bring your focus deep into your heart. Noticing the left and right sides as they contract and expand, contract and expand, contract and expand out with blood and fresh energy. Contracting and then enlarging once more.

Bring your attention to the bottom and back of your heart. Do you notice the sweetness that exists at the back of your heart, deep in its center? Beyond the contraction, beyond the breath. Allow your mind and imagination to dive deeply into that sweet, deep, rich center of your heart.

Notice how your breath may have calmed and evened out the longer you pay attention to your heartbeat. You may notice that your heartbeat is spreading more widely. You may feel it's filling your entire chest as you become even more deeply aware of the area in the back of your heart.

You may feel an increasing warmth and calm and sweetness. Allow your breathing to be easy.

Give yourself another several rounds of breath. Simply being with your heart, appreciating how hard it's beating. How consistently and how much sweetness are there in its depths.

Allow yourself a few more rounds of breath to appreciate the experience of your own heartbeat. When you feel complete, go on about your day. I wish you well.

You can download the audio of this meditation at AnUnstoppableLife.com.

Spiral of Breath

A meditation for loosening the entire body and building subtle energy.

Settle into your seat. Feel free to move around a little as you settle in, shaking out your arms and legs, shoulders, hips, and ribcage. Give your neck a few rolls around in one direction and then reverse.

Slowly start to spiral your body, from your hip bones all the way up to the top of your head, allowing all the parts of your body from your hips upward to spiral at their own pace. You might start with a quick spiral and move slowly. You might start with a slow one and quicken it as you go. Allow the spiral to take on its own shape and flavor.

You can start with all the parts of your torso moving as one. Notice that as they warm, they start to move at their own pace, creating a series of smaller spirals linked almost like looking at an external version of DNA. Allow the movement to find its own rhythm and its own pace, and notice what direction the spiral is in without needing to change anything.

Allow the muscles in your entire torso to loosen even more. The spiral becomes its own dance, its own breath.

If emotions bubble up, or thoughts arise, imagine them spiraling all the way out and up, out of your head, right into the sky. Breathing as easily and gently and quickly as feels right to you in this moment.

If thoughts and emotions come up, does your spiral change? How quickly can you let go of thinking the thoughts or getting caught in the emotions? Once again, imagine breathing them up and out this top of the spiral.

Whatever direction you have been spiraling in, take a deep breath in stillness and spiral in the opposite direction. Moving in a way that may feel awkward in the beginning. As you very gently unwind the spiral of breath that you have been creating. You may notice that you feel as though you're hunkering down and reconnecting with the earth where it might have felt in the beginning that you were spiraling upward and reaching for the sky.

Perhaps you started by reconnecting with the earth and grounding, and now you're lengthening upward. Whatever direction you find yourself spiraling in is perfect.

Know that each time that you practice, you may find yourself starting in a different direction. Trust that your body is leading you in the direction it needs to wind and unwind. There is no right or wrong way to spiral.

Let your breath be easy as you spiral in this second direction. Again, notice if emotions or thoughts arise. Can you let them go at the end or at the peak of your spiral, releasing them down into the earth or upward into the sky? Clearing your entire system and your physical body, the entire spiral of your DNA, of anything that can be released right now.

As you settle into the last minute, the last full 60 seconds of this practice, find your way to stillness.

Notice that as you bring your body to a central point, you may feel as though you're a bit suspended between source and earth, between sky and ground.

You may feel weightless. You may feel fully grounded. Simply notice what absolute stillness and breath feel like this last 30 seconds.

Allow yourself to remain in this stillness of breath, the stillness of breathing for as long as you would like in your practice today. I wish you well for the rest of your day.

You can download the audio of this meditation at AnUnstoppableLife.com.

Best Self Exercise

Time Required

You'll experience the most benefit if you practice this for 15 minutes every day for two weeks.

How to Do It

Take a moment to imagine your life in the future. What is the best possible life you can imagine? Consider all the relevant areas of your life, such as your career, academic work, relationships, hobbies, and/or health. What happens while you live your best possible future?

For the next 15 minutes, write continuously about what you imagine this best possible future to be. Use the instructions on the next page to help guide you through this process.

1. It's easy to start comparing your current life to your best possible future. You might start thinking about how accomplishing goals has been difficult for you, or about financial/time/social barriers. I encourage you to focus firmly on your future—imagine a bright future in which you're your best self and your circumstances change just enough to make this best possible life real.

2. This exercise is most useful when you get very specific—if you think about a new job, imagine exactly what you would do, who you would work with, and where it would be. The more specific you are, the more engaged you'll be in the exercise and the more you'll get out of it.

3. Be as creative and imaginative as you want and don't worry about grammar, spelling, or form.

You can draw Venn diagrams, write in bullet points or prose. Whatever allows your ideas to flow freely—do that.

How to Keep a Journal

Notes for starting and keeping a journal.

1. Get a journal you like! Whether it's hand-bound and hand-made, spiral-bound plain paper, or legal pad, it should inspire you to hold it and open it. If gridded pages turn you on, get a notebook with a grid, if you like wide-open spaces for doodling, then get a blank book without lines at all. The key is that you should have a journal that you enjoy looking at and working in.

2. It doesn't have to look like anything in particular! You can write notes or jot ideas, draw pictures or doodle, make lists or use different colors of ink. You can add articles and pictures to visualize ideas and clarify goals. Whatever it looks like is totally up to you. It's your journal, so don't play by anyone else's rules, really make it your own.

3. Find time to write each day! Fifteen minutes in the morning, at lunch, or in the evening—whatever works best for you is the right time.

4. Record events and ideas as they happen! Try not to wait until later to write. Our brains are really good at forgetting how we were feeling. Record emotions and details regularly and you'll form the most useful information bank for yourself.

5. Read your journal! Yes, I know you wrote it... but reviewing what you wrote it the way you'll make use of the information you gather. At the end of the week, read each day's entry. Ask yourself some questions about what you notice. How was your mood? Did it fluctuate a lot or a little? Did the weather affect you, your mood, or your activity level? Did something unexpected happen during the week? At the end of each month, go back and do a quick review of the month; what do you notice about how things flowed this month? How does that compare to last month, or to several months ago?

Reading your journal is really helpful to do if you're doing the WWW+W exercise. Reviewing that record of daily "what went well and why" can help you ground in your actions and solidify the new, positive habits that help you create and reach your goals.

What Went Well and Why

Set aside about ten minutes before you go to sleep. In two sentences for each, write three things that went well today and why they went well. You can use a journal, your computer, or voice notes on your phone.

The three items don't need to be of the highest importance (*My boyfriend brought my favorite fruit on the way home today*), and they can be simple (*It was a sunny day*).

For each positive event, answer the question *Why did this happen?* For example, if you wrote that your boyfriend brought you a treat, you might write *because my boyfriend is thoughtful,* or *because I texted him to ask if he could pick some up for me*. If you write, *It was a sunny day*, you might note the cause as, *I took time to notice that it was sunny*. The WHY in each case is how you affected the positive event or outcome. Sometimes this will be because you took time to notice something good, or because you allowed yourself time to choose an action that resulted in a more positive outcome. In each case, consider how something you did, thought, or felt resulted in a positive event or outcome.

Noticing **why** the positive events in your life happen may feel awkward at first, and I invite you to experiment for an entire week. It gets to be more fun as you go. The best news is that people who do this practice every day for at least 3 weeks see a measurable decrease in depression, symptoms of physical illness, and an increased sense of wellbeing and connectedness.

Visual Meditation Practice

Use the mandala* here, or another one you like, and allow yourself time to meditate on the design as you trace it with your fingers, eyes or color it in.

* My thanks to Tom Cornish for his glorious designs.

Meditation Mandala 1

Meditation Mandala 2

Core Values List

Acceptance	Brilliance	Competence
Accomplishment	Calm	Concentration
Accountability	Candor	Confidence
Accuracy	Capable	Connection
Achievement	Careful	Consciousness
Adaptability	Certainty	Consistency
Alertness	Challenge	Contentment
Altruism	Charity	Contribution
Ambition	Cleanliness	Control
Amusement	Clear	Conviction
Assertiveness	Clever	Cooperation
Attentive	Comfort	Courage
Awareness	Commitment	Courtesy
Balance	Common sense	Creation
Beauty	Communication	Creativity
Boldness	Community	Credibility
Bravery	Compassion	Curiosity

Decisive	Generosity	Logic
Dedication	Genius	Love
Dependability	Giving	Loyalty
Determination	Goodness	Mastery
Development	Grace	Maturity
Devotion	Gratitude	Meaning
Dignity	Greatness	Moderation
Discipline	Growth	Motivation
Discovery	Happiness	Openness
Drive	Hard work	Optimism
Effectiveness	Harmony	Order
Efficiency	Health	Organization
Empathy	Honesty	Originality
Empower	Honor	Passion
Endurance	Hope	Patience
Energy	Humility	Peace
Enjoyment	Imagination	Performance
Enthusiasm	Improvement	Persistence
Equality	Independence	Playfulness
Ethical	Individuality	Poise
Excellence	Innovation	Potential
Experience	Inquisitive	Power
Exploration	Insightful	Present
Expressive	Inspiring	Productivity
Fairness	Integrity	Professionalism
Family	Intelligence	Prosperity
Famous	Intensity	Purpose
Fearless	Intuitive	Quality
Feelings	Irreverent	Realistic
Ferocious	Joy	Reason
Fidelity	Justice	Recognition
Focus	Kindness	Recreation
Foresight	Knowledge	Reflective
Fortitude	Lawful	Respect
Freedom	Leadership	Responsibility
Friendship	Learning	Restraint
Fun	Liberty	Results-oriented

Reverence
Rigor
Risk
Satisfaction
Security
Self-reliance
Selfless
Sensitivity
Serenity
Service
Sharing
Significance
Silence
Simplicity
Sincerity
Skill
Skillfulness
Smart
Solitude
Spirit
Spirituality
Spontaneous
Stability
Status
Stewardship
Strength
Structure
Success
Support
Surprise
Sustainability
Talent
Teamwork
Temperance
Thankful
Thorough
Thoughtful

Timeliness
Tolerant
Toughness
Traditional
Tranquility
Transparency
Trust
Trustworthy
Truth
Understanding
Uniqueness
Unity
Valor
Victory
Vigor
Vision
Vitality
Wealth
Welcoming
Winning
Wisdom
Wonder

List of Human Emotions

(ACCORDING TO THE DISCRETE EMOTION THEORY)

Just like worldviews, there are several theories of emotion. I'm giving you what I hope is the most straightforward list. The idea is that emotions are separate, discrete things and that they are "basic" because they exist from us having to deal with fundamental life tasks, like avoiding speeding cars or running away from tigers. This theory starts with these five basic emotions and then expands each one by varying degrees of intensity.

BASIC EMOTIONS AND THEIR RELATED FEELINGS:

Enjoyment:
- pleasure
- joy
- happiness
- amusement
- pride
- awe
- excitement
- ecstasy

Sadness:
- lonely
- unhappy
- hopeless
- gloomy
- miserable

Fear:
- worried
- nervous
- anxious
- scared
- panicked
- stressed

Anger:
- annoyed
- frustrated
- bitter
- infuriated
- mad
- insulted
- vengeful

Disgust:
- dislike
- revulsion
- nauseated
- aversion
- offended
- horrified

Write Your Personal Manifesto: Worksheet

Start with five minutes of writing. You can always write more if you want to.

Write without too much concern about what comes out on the page, then review what you've written and highlight the statements that you feel most passionate about.

Take a few deep breaths and think back over your life. Touch on challenges you've met, goals you've reached, failures that have taught you valuable lessons. Notice who you were being in those moments. What were you doing, what actions did you take or choose not to take?

What types of challenges are you drawn to in life? What do you gravitate towards? What are the core values that make you who you are? What themes or situations show up for you?

Take a few minutes to reflect on where you feel powerful, vulnerable, at ease, and most yourself. You're more than someone who is driven by money or success, what other areas of your life have made you who you're today? What empowers you, what drives you?

What do you know is true and what do you believe in?

You can start with:

I believe in...

I know this is true...

I create... in the world.

Living an Unstoppable Life Cheat Sheet

1. Open two bank accounts, one for necessities and one so you can save for the "fun stuff" in life.

2. Do a serious spring cleaning on your whole life at least once a year. Clear out old items from your house, old ideas from your mind, and old habits that no longer serve you.

3. Make a list of the ten things that make you deep down, dancing-around-the-living-room happy.

4. Buy one cookbook that inspires you and cook your way through it over the course of a year.

5. Learn to change a car tire, even if you don't have a car.

6. Do one thing a day that makes you laugh out loud.

7. Learn to read a paper map correctly.

8. Learn to drive a manual transmission car.

9. Learn how to make an omelet.

10. Take two minutes and dance around your kitchen at least once a week.

11. Go for a walk and simply listen to what the world really sounds like.

12. Spend 2 minutes each day appreciating the sky.

13. Learn to read a compass.

14. Learn to read a ruler.

15. Learn a foreign language.

16. Pay for a stranger's coffee or tea.

17. Hold the door open for a stranger and smile.

18. Cut yourself some slack when you are having a really bad day.

19. Have at least one really good, sharp knife in your kitchen.

20. Learn to sew.

21. Read a poem out loud once a week.

22. Sing your favorite song at the top of your lungs.

23. Own a decent jacket.

24. Toss out socks with holes in them (or learn to darn them).

25. Clear out any clothes you haven't worn in 2 years.

26. Be willing to be silly.

27. Laugh at yourself.

28. Trust your intuition.

29. Learn one new fact every week.

30. Don't let laundry or frustrations pile up.

31. Splash in the nearest stream, pond, ocean, or lake.

32. Take yourself on a date.

33. Write a love letter to yourself.

34. Clear out clothes that make you feel like someone else.

35. Let your home be a haven.

36. Buy flowers for yourself.

37. Treat yourself to something that makes you giggle and costs less than $5.00.

38. Put away electronics at least one hour before bedtime, for better sleep.

39. Make S'mores for absolutely no reason.

40. Get the T.V. or screen out of your bedroom.

41. Trust that who you are is worthy of love.

42. Create a "Joy Jar" of daily accomplishments.

43. Finger-paint.

44. Invite a friend for a walk, bike ride, or hike.

45. Bundle up, bring hot cocoa, and sit on a beach in winter.

46. Do one thing that stretches your mind every day.

47. Stretch your body for five minutes every day.

48. Practice push-ups until you can easily do 50 without stopping.

49. Change your toothbrush every six months.

50. Have one computer-free day every week.

51. Stop working weekends.

52. Don't talk baby-talk to kids.

53. If something feels impossible, break it down into smaller action steps.

54. Learn to be alone. Practice until you can happily be alone for a day or more.

55. Trim your eyebrows.

56. Don't wear shoes you can't walk a mile in.

57. Give yourself 72 hours before you try to solve a problem.

58. Be gracious to yourself and others.

59. Allow yourself an extra fifteen minutes to get anywhere.

60. Be five minutes early for meetings.

61. Be fifteen minutes late for dinner parties.

62. Don't bring chips of any kind to a potluck.

63. Change your socks.

64. Find a color that makes you happy and wear it more often.

65. Dance while you walk your dog.

66. Lie under the stars once a week.

67. Practice holding elbow plank pose for at least two minutes a day.

68. Take seven minutes of deep inhaling and exhaling before you get out of bed in the morning.

69. Let yourself sleep in at least once a week.

70. Go to a county fair and ride the Ferris wheel and carousel.

71. Remember you don't have to fix everything.

72. Don't share personal news or information that isn't yours.

73. Let your friends know you value them.

74. Don't ghost people.

75. Invite someone on a picnic.

76. Set aside some money each week, even if it's $10.00, then invest it after six months. Repeat twice a year.

77. Watch more comedy.

78. Have a civil conversation with someone you disagree with and really listen.

79. Blow soap bubbles.

80. Remember you are the creator of your own happiness.

81. Choose work that you love and that excites something in you.

82. If you are bored at work, find some way to make it more interesting, challenging and productive.

83. Cook dinner for friends.

84. If you hate cooking, then throw a potluck gathering.

85. Not everything needs a response.

86. Be generous and honest with your praise.

87. Take time each day to name one thing that went well that day.

88. Treat your family and friends with respect.

89. Be creative in problem-solving.

90. Remember, your romantic partner is not your "be-all-and-end-all," they are human.

91. No job is beneath you.

92. Whatever you do, give it your all, every time.

93. Life is messy, the messier the more alive.

94. Grief is personal—take your time and find your own way through it, no matter what everyone around you thinks.

95. Substitute fruit for sugary snacks.

96. Allow yourself to be surprised.

97. Ask, "What's the best that could happen?"

98. Check in with how you are feeling.

99. Keep your daily "to-do" list to three items.

100. Write yourself a love note on your bathroom mirror.

101. Tell one person a day something you appreciate about them.

102. Try one new thing a month even if it's an epic failure.

103. Learn to balance on one foot with your eyes closed.

104. Wash your face, brush your teeth and fix your hair every day.

105. Socks don't have to match every time.

106. Toss holey underwear.

107. Try not to spend any money for a day, a week, or a month.

108. Face your fears—they are not silly, but they might be getting in your way.

109. Write a personal mission statement.

110. Clearly define your top five personal core values.

111. Learn to apologize thoughtfully.

112. Don't make excuses.

113. Stop saying "just."

114. Be considerate and open doors for others.

115. Own your mistakes.

116. Failure leads to success when you keep working

117. Pick up trash when you are out walking.

118. Have an ice cream.

119. Be honest and tactful.

120. Thank yourself daily for something you did.

121. Get enough sleep, whatever "enough" is for you.

122. Take a vacation of some kind, even if it's one day.

123. Breathe deeply when waves of strong emotions overtake you.

124. Practice seeing the people you know well as though for the first time.

125. Ask yourself how you can respect yourself in one specific action each day.

126. Replace "but" with "and..." and see what happens.

127. Remember you don't have to say yes to everything.

128. Meet problems gently, and head-on.

129. Accept compliments wholeheartedly.

130. Learn to listen and compromise.

131. Lean into your own strengths.

132. Remember all the experiences you have gathered in life.

133. Don't ask "Why?" Ask "What?" or "How?"

134. Think of ten things you're grateful for and name them out loud.

135. Write a letter of gratitude to someone and read it or send it to them.

136. Learn the lyrics to a new song.

137. Volunteer to help someone this week.

138. Allow courage to surface.

139. Being vulnerable is a strength.

140. Learn to whistle.

141. Pay attention to what your heart truly wants to create.

142. Find a new route to work or for your next dog walk.

143. Meet at least one other person for socializing each week.

144. Create a ritual for yourself to release old habits that don't serve you.

145. Buy a helium balloon, smile, and give it to the first person you meet.

146. Explore something near where you live, that is totally unknown to you.

147. Take an art class—even if you *think* you aren't artistic.

148. Grab a friend and go to a new social meet-up.

149. Trust that we get to be silly and most people won't even notice.

150. Give up caffeine for a week and see how you feel.

151. Learn to type better.

152. Put at least one game on your smartphone.

153. Practice forward folds so you can touch your toes easily every morning.

154. Take a one-minute cold shower every day.

155. Get a pedicure at least once in your life.

156. Get a really fancy manicure at least once in your life.

157. Treat yourself to a hotel breakfast even if it's in the town you live in.

158. Travel at least 300 miles from where you live once a year.

159. Get a physical check-up once a year.

160. Check your vitamin D levels.

161. Remember that everyone looks weird on video calls at one point or another.

162. Dress to impress yourself.

163. Write a poem.

164. Keep a gratitude journal for a month and notice what changes in your life.

165. Use moisturizer and sunblock 365 days a year, even if you are inside most of the day.

166. Wake up to a song you love and dance while brushing your teeth.

167. Bike or walk to work if you can.

168. Find something to laugh at every day.

169. Enjoy sex.

170. Trust your heart.

171. Clean behind your fridge and oven.

172. Try time-blocking your weekly schedule to better balance work and fun.

173. Forgive your parents.

174. Forgive yourself.

175. Wear something that makes you feel amazing at least once a week.

176. Train your puppy.

177. Don't mix light and dark clothes in the wash.

178. Smile at strangers

179. Read a book for fun at least once every two months.

180. Buy flowers at the grocery store and hand them to the person who checks out after you.

181. Accept that no one is perfect.

182. Ask your friends to tell you five things they love about you.

183. Tell your friends six things you love about them.

184. Don't argue when someone compliments you.

185. Remember, guilt moves us to action, shame stops us in our tracks.

186. You are not your parents.

187. Choose what life you want to create for yourself.

188. When you get stuck, ask yourself what you'd advise your BFF to do.

189. Practice handstands.

190. Let yourself enjoy life.

191. Have a pocket knife and corkscrew handy.

192. Forgive your siblings.

193. Remember that you are responsible for your own happiness.

194. Let others be who they are.

195. If your dog barks for more than eight minutes, bring her inside.

196. Plant wildflowers wherever you can.

197. Do something that scares you a bit, every six months.

198. If you think you can't... you won't.

199. Ask for more hugs.

200. Let your heart shine big and bright in the world, whatever that looks like for you!

Acknowledgments

This handbook for creating an unstoppable life was born from the realization that much of what has led me to live an adventurous and successful life has been the knowledge my father, Neil, taught me, 90% by virtue of doing rather than telling.

Often, he'd launch my brother or me into a project or task without any preamble or explanation except to tell us what tools to grab from the workshop or studio. The projects varied from re-roofing the house to building RC-model planes, getting eggs or a chicken from the farm down the road, or learning how to use and sharpen any number of hand tools.

I'm forever grateful he taught me the seemingly random and completely practical set of skills I now pass along to you in much the same way... though you'll have to read them unless you invite me out for a weekend adventure.

I'm also grateful to Dylan Brody and his Saturday Writer's

group. Without their encouragement and keen ears, this book would never have seen the light of day, much less the ink on paper. Also, thanks to the kind friends who acted as readers and helped me mold the mess of essays into coherent form. Many thanks as well to the kind people at various coffeeshops who salved my spirits with great cups of java and tables to write when I couldn't stand being at my home desk another minute.

And a final appreciation to my dog and cat who often snoozed and snored comfortingly under my feet on long writing days when I might otherwise have lost hope of finishing this book.

~Amrita Rose

About Atmosphere Press

Atmosphere Press is an independent, full-service publisher for excellent books in all genres and for all audiences. Learn more about what we do at atmospherepress.com.

We encourage you to check out some of Atmosphere's latest releases, which are available at Amazon.com and via order from your local bookstore:

The Ideological and Political System of Banselism, by Royard Halmonet Vantion (Ancheng Wang)

Nursing Homes: A Missionary's Journey Through Heaven's Waiting Room, by Tim Eatman, Ph.D.

Timeline of Stars, by Joe Adcock

A Boy Who Loved Me, by Wilson Semitti

The Injustice in Justice, by Charmaine Loverin

Living in the Grey, by Katie Weber

Living with Veracity, Dying with Dignity, by Alison Clay-Duboff

Noah's Rejects, by Rob Kagan

A lot of Questions (with no answers)?, by Jordan Neben

Cowboy from Prague: An Immigrant's Pursuit of the American Dream, by Charles Ota Heller

Sleeping under the bridge, by Melissa Baker

The only prayer I ever have to say is thank you, by M. Kaya Hill

Amygdala Blue, by Paul Lomax

A Caregiver's Love Story, by Nancie Wiseman Attwater

Taming Infection: The American Response to Illness from Smallpox to Covid, by Gregg Coodley and David Sarasohn

Me & Mrs Jones, by Justine Glassen

About the Author

Writer, Life & Career Coach, Akashic worker, Artist and all-around Provocateur Amrita Rose has navigated three major (and many minor) career changes, lived in two countries and seven states, and continues to plan her next adventures. She has garnered enthusiastic appreciation for her community-based programs of yoga, meditation, integrated art practices and Positive Psychology "Positivity Slams", all of which have enhanced the lives and not depleted the pockets of diverse groups of attendees.

Amrita skillfully weaves her deep knowledge of Yogic Science, Pranayama, various forms of meditation, along with a background in education, clinical mental health, Positive Psychology and more esoteric mindful and spiritual practices. She developed one of the most highly regarded yoga and meditation programs for in-patient mental health clinics and notable lowered the return rate of patients by more than 50% in the first year.

Doing her best writing while camping, hiking, and cabin-sitting, or perched atop a coffee-shop stool or a rocky mountain, Amrita loves to educate and inspire...motivating readers to be bold and dive into the work of honest transformation in their lives. She offers lived experience and wisdom garnered from hard work, and taking a no B.S. approach to herself and to life in general and encourages clients and readers to do the same!

Want FREEBIES to inspire you?
Sign up for her newsletter at
https://AnUnstoppableLife.com/